# *The* Asbury *Journal*

# SPRING 1995

# VOL.50 . NO.1

# *The*Asbury*Journal*

**EDITOR**
Robert Danielson

**EDITORIAL BOARD**
Kenneth J. Collins
*Professor of Historical Theology and Wesley Studies*
J. Steven O'Malley
*Professor of Methodist Holiness History*

**EDITORIAL ADVISORY PANEL**
William Abraham, *Perkins School of Theology*
David Bundy, *New York Theological Seminary*
Ted Campbell, *Perkins School of Theology*
Hyungkeun Choi, *Seoul Theological University*
Richard Heitzenrater, *Duke University Divinity School*
Scott Kisker, *Wesley Theological Seminary*
Sarah Lancaster, *Methodist Theological School of Ohio*
Gareth Lloyd, *University of Manchester*
Randy Maddox, *Duke University Divinity School*
Nantachai Medjuhon, *Muang Thai Church, Bangkok, Thailand*
Stanley Nwoji, *Pastor, Lagos, Nigeria*
Paul Numrich, *Theological Consortium of Greater Columbus*
Dana Robert, *Boston University*
Howard Snyder, *Manchester Wesley Research Centre*
L. Wesley de Souza, *Candler School of Theology*
Leonard Sweet, *Drew University School of Theology*
Amos Yong, *Regent University*
Hwa Yung, *United Methodist Church, Kuala Lampur, Malaysia*

All inquiries regarding subscriptions, back issues, permissions to reprint, manuscripts for submission, and books for review should be addressed to:

**The Asbury Journal**
Asbury Theological Seminary
204 N. Lexington Avenue, Wilmore, KY 40390
FAX: 859-858-2375
http://place.asburyseminary.edu/asburyjournal/
© Copyright 2020 by Asbury Theological Seminary

# THE
## ASBURY THEOLOGICAL
# JOURNAL

Asbury Theological Seminary
204 N. Lexington Avenue
Wilmore, KY 40390-1199

# THE
# ASBURY THEOLOGICAL
# JOURNAL

SPRING 1995                    Volume 50, Number 1

Theology of Creation and Natural Science ...............................5
  *Wolfhart Pannenberg*

The Emergence of Creatures and Their Succession in a
Developing Universe ...............................................................17
  *Wolfhart Pannenberg*

Christianity and Secularism .....................................................27
  *Wolfhart Pannenberg*

The Sabbath-Rest of the Maker of All .......................................37
  *Stanley L. Jaki*

On the Legality and Morality of
Physician-Assisted Suicide ......................................................51
  *David J. Baggett*

Theological Education After Communism:
The Mixed Blessing of Western Assistance ...............................67
  *Mark Elliott*

The Soteriological Orientation of
John Wesley's Ministry to the Poor...........................................75
  *Kenneth J. Collins*

Book Reviews .........................................................................93

# THE
# ASBURY THEOLOGICAL
# JOURNAL

SPRING 1995                                    Volume 50, Number 1

Theology of Creation and Natural Science ............................................................5
    Wolfhart Pannenberg

The Emergence of Creatures and Their Succession
in a Developing Universe .................................................................................17
    Wolfhart Pannenberg

Christianity and Secularism ..............................................................................27
    Wolfhart Pannenberg

The Sabbath-Rest of the Maker of All ...............................................................37
    Stanley L. Jaki

On the Legality and Morality of
Physician-Assisted Suicide ...............................................................................51
    David J. Baggett

Theological Education After Communism:
The Mixed Blessing of Western Assistance ........................................................67
    Mark Elliott

The Soteriological Orientation of
John Wesley's Ministry to the Poor ..................................................................75
    Kenneth J. Collins

Book Reviews ..................................................................................................93
Jaroslav Pelikan, *Christianity and Classical Culture. The Metamorphosis of Natural
    Theology in the Christian Encounter with Hellenism* [David Bundy]
Charles S. McCoy and J. Wayne Baker, *Fountainhead of Federalism: Heinrich
    Bullinger and the Covenantal Tradition* [Marc Clauson]
Russell E. Richey, *Early American Methodism* [Roderick T. Leupp]
Kenneth D. Gill, *Toward a Contextualized Theology for the Third World* [David
    Bundy]
Karla Poewe, ed., *Charismatic Christianity as a Global Culture* [David Bundy]

# THE
# ASBURY THEOLOGICAL
# JOURNAL

Published in April and October by
Asbury Theological Seminary.
**Postmaster**: Send address changes to:
The Asbury Theological Journal
Asbury Theological Seminary
204 North Lexington Avenue
Wilmore, KY 40390

USPS 547-440
Continuing *The Asbury Seminarian*

Printed in the U.S.A.

THE ASBURY THEOLOGICAL JOURNAL provides a scholarly forum for thorough discussion of issues relevant to Christian thought and faith, and to the nature and mission of the Church. *The Journal* addresses those concerns and ideas across the curriculum which interface with Christian thought, life, and ministry.

The primary resource for contributions to *The Journal* is the Asbury Seminary faculty who engage in dialogue with both the roots of our religious heritage and contemporary thought. Scholars from other academic disciplines and various backgrounds are invited to submit articles for publication.

The positions espoused in articles in *The Journal* do not necessarily represent the views of the editors or of Asbury Theological Seminary.

Books for review and articles for consideration should be mailed to: Scott R. Burson, Asbury Theological Seminary, Wilmore, KY 40390-1199 (telephone: 606-858-3581). Manuscripts should be in English and typed double-spaced on white bond paper, 8 1/2 x 11 inches. Send only original copies (not photocopies) with an accompanying computer disk (3.5 inch) whenever possible. Acceptance for publication will be acknowledged and will obligate the author to submit a 100-word abstract; in return, a modest honorarium payment will follow publication. Sermons, poetry and devotional material are not used. Unsolicited manuscripts will not be returned unless a self-addressed envelope with sufficient postage is provided. Queries are welcome, and a style sheet is available upon request.

Articles in *The Journal* are indexed in *The Christian Periodical Index* and *Religion Index One: Periodicals (RIO)*; book reviews are indexed in *Index to Book Reviews in Religion (IBRR)*. Both *RIO* and *IBRR* are published by the American Theological Library Association, 5600 South Woodlawn Avenue, Chicago, IL 60637, and are available online through BRS Information Technologies and DIALOG Information Services. Articles, starting with vol. 43, are abstracted in *Religious and Theological Abstracts*. Articles in appropriate categories are also abstracted in *Old Testament Abstracts* and *New Testament Abstracts*.

Volumes in microform of *The Asbury Theological Journal* (vols. 41-) and *The Asbury Seminarian* (vols. 1-40) are available from University Microfilms International, 300 North Zeeb Road, Ann Arbor, MI 48106.

Articles and Reviews may be copied for personal or internal use, and permission to reprint all or portions of any of the contents may be granted upon request to the managing editor.

## SUBSCRIPTIONS:

One year (2 issues), $5.00
(outside the U.S., $8.00)
Two years, $8.00 ($14.00)
Three years, $11.00 ($20.00)

# THEOLOGY OF CREATION
# AND NATURAL SCIENCE

WOLFHART PANNENBERG

Half a century ago Karl Barth wrote in the preface to his treatment of creation in his *Church Dogmatics* (III/1, 1945), that there are "absolutely no scientific questions, objections or supports concerning what Scripture and the Christian Church understand to be God's work of creation." Such a restriction of the theology of creation to a "retelling" of what the Bible tells us about this subject, has its price and the price to be paid here was that it could no longer be made clear, in how far the biblical faith in creation means the same world that the human race now inhabits and that is described by modern science. The affirmation that the God of the Bible created the world degenerates into an empty formula, and the biblical God himself becomes a powerless phantom, if he can no longer be understood as the one who originates and completes the world as it is given to our experience. For this reason one should not agree with Barth, but rather with Karl Heim in his attempt to relate theological affirmations on creation and final consummation of the world to the respective conceptions of contemporary science (1953). In the context of English theology a theological appropriation of Darwin's doctrine of evolution was developed as soon as 1889 in the famous volume *Lux Mundi*, edited by Charles Gorn, where the biblical conception of a history of salvation culminating in the event of incarnation was combined with the modern evolutionary perspective, and this view has been effective until the present day together with related ideas issuing from the work of Teilhard de Chardin.

In spite of all the difficulties of a theological interpretation of the natural

*Wolfhart Pannenberg is Professor Emeritus of Systematic Theology at the University of Munich. These three papers were delivered at Asbury Theological Seminary in the spring of 1994.*

world, Christian theology must not evade the task of interpreting the same world that is described by scientists to be in fact the creation of God. It is not enough to simply affirm the world to be God's creation, but such a theological affirmation has to be made plausible. This is not to suggest that theology should enter the discussions among scientists on their level of scientific description and theory. Theological interpretation of the world of nature in terms of creation cannot want to present itself as competing with physics or with any other natural science. Claims like that are excluded by the fact that theological arguments move on another methodological level than the hypotheses of natural law in the sciences and their examination by experiment do. From a theological perspective the reality of the world presents itself in the form of a unique and irreversible historical process which is the result and expression of divine action. Certainly, in the process of this history there emerge uniformities and structural types of sequences of natural events that correspond to the scientific concept of natural law. In the book of Genesis it said after the story on the flood: "While the earth remains, seedtime and harvest, cold and heat, summer and winter, day and night, shall not cease" (Gen. 8:22). Such regularities of natural processes, however, are themselves considered as products of a unique divine decision, not as evidence of a timeless order of nature. The theological focus on the historically unique and on the irreversible process of history is also related to the fact that theology does not conceive of space and time in the sense of homogeneous sequences of spatial and temporal units—sequences that can be geometrically constructed, counted, and measured. The mathematical form of representing and describing natural processes and the scientific concept of law belong together. The absence of mathematical descriptions in theology, on the other hand, does not only express the inability of theologians, but also corresponds to the peculiarity of the theological subject matter and its appropriate treatment.

Now the question arises, whether theology exemplifies a qualitative way of describing reality, such as has been so often reduced in the history of modern science to a quantitative and consequently mathematical way of description. The ideas of the biblical reports on creation about the sequence in the emergence of natural forms have been indeed replaced in modern science by conceptions which are based on quantitative descriptions of processes regulated by natural law. Should this tendency be generally valid concerning the relationship between theology and science? The American physicist Frank Tipler of New Orleans claims in his recent book, *The Physics of Immortality*, that theology finally has to be absorbed in physics. In his book, he tries to show that the history of the universe tends towards an omega point, which is characterized by peculiar properties of the traditional concept of God and does not only function as the result, but also as creative origin of the movement of the universe, and there is occasion for an identical repetition of all forms of intelligent life in the dimension of eternity. Professor Tipler accounts for these claims by a proposed theory of scientific cosmology. The educated layman cannot help being impressed, but he or she is also impressed by the multitude of different models of scientific cosmology produced over the last decades. Cosmology, to all appearance, is a highly speculative discipline. But how is theology to be expected to relate to the possibility of those arguments?

I think that attempted transformations of theology into physics should be observed with curiosity on the one hand, but also with a certain degree of skepticism on the other. Curiosity and openness are appropriate, since even tentative constructions of this kind of work against the widespread prejudice that theological and scientific conceptions are unrelated—a prejudice the effect of which is usually that theology seems to be irrelevant concerning our understanding of the reality we inhabit. Skepticism, however, is appropriate because of the apparent incommensurability between the scientific conception of natural law and the theological approach to reality. Could indeed the conception of the world in terms of a unique and irreversible history of ever new and contingent events including the idea of God providing their origin, and of Christian eschatological hope, be dissolved without important remnant into a description of the world process on the basis of natural law? Even at this point I see no basis for theological anxieties. After all, there is the historical parallel of Aristotelian physics, the objects of which included the existence of God, though not of a future resurrection of the dead. A proper conception of God as creative origin of the natural universe, to be sure, had to describe the creation of the world by starting from God as origin of it rather than dealing with God as an exponent of the cosmic process. In Christian theology, such a comprehensive knowledge of creation that would comprise all the different aspects of created reality is not expected before the final consummation of the world in connection with the eschatological vision of the glorified ones. Until then it seems likely that human knowledge about the world will develop under conditions of human finitude and therefore in the form of conjectures only and by way of their examination and revision. In a reverse argument, Christian theology seeks to conceive of God as creator of the world on the basis of His revelation in Jesus Christ. But in doing this, theology is not in a position to explain in detail the processes in the natural world.

The aim of reaching an agreement between the theology of creation on the one hand and the scientific knowledge about the world of nature on the other, may be indicated, then, more properly by the term consonance between the two perspectives than by way of reducing one of them to the other. Consonance presupposes the absence of contradiction. But it requires more than that. Contradictions can be absent, simply because ideas stand unrelated, one beside the other. Consonance, however, implies the image of some harmony and consequently of a positive relationship. How can such a consonance be claimed with respect to affirmations that belong to quite different methodological levels? In such a case, it is necessary to look for a third level, which the two others are related to. In the case of the dialog between science and theology such a third level has indeed always existed. It is the level of philosophy.

Whenever scientists talk about the relevance of their findings and theoretical formulas in view of our understanding of reality, they move in the medium of philosophical reflection on procedures and results of their science, but no longer on the level of scientific argument in the strict sense. Reflections on the relationship between natural law and the contingency of events, between causality and freedom, matter and energy, the concepts of time and space or evolution take place inevitably in a medium that is impregnated with philosophical language and its history. Furthermore, in most cases the key concepts of science have philosophical origins and underwent modifications in order to fit the requirements of their use in science. Recent investigations into the history of scientific concepts like space, time, mass, force, and field demonstrated connections between the philosophical meaning of these concepts and their scientific use. Therefore, together with familiarity with the philosophical discussions on these subjects, a degree of knowledge in the history of science and especially about the history of scientific terminology, is a presupposition of a productive dialog between theology and the sciences.

Christian theology, on the other hand, in the entire course of its history, developed in close connection with philosophy, though the relationship was not without its complications and strains. In the case of theology and in distinction from the sciences, the relationship to philosophy is not, in the first place, a matter of philosophical origins of a particular terminology, but rather the task of integrating into theology and into its explication of the relation of God the creator and redeemer of the world and of humanity the philosophical language about God, the world, and the place of human beings in it. Such integration of philosophical theses and conceptions into Christian theology always meant a more or less incisive transformation of the philosophical meaning, and the occasional tensions arising between theology and philosophy in the course of history often arose from such attempts at appropriation. Theology, however, is affirming the abiding truth of the biblical God and of His revelation as concerning every human being always depended and will depend on rational universality of philosophy and therefore had to assimilate to itself not only the philosophical doctrines on God, but also the philosophical affirmations on the world and human beings. At this point it finally becomes apparent in how far for Christian theology the relationship to the philosophical interpretation of the world becomes the basis of a dialog with the sciences: the inclusion of scientific considerations and results in a reflection on how to perceive of reality at large and of the situation of human beings in the world is not the first and only subject of a theological doctrine of creation, but belonged always to the philosophical interpretation of the world we encounter. In dealing with its task of critical appropriation and assimilation of a philosophical view of the world, theology implicitly dealt always with the knowledge of nature it contained, and on the other hand the theological transformation of philosophical concepts of the world has to be measured like philosophical hypotheses themselves by their ability to do justice to scientific views and results.

Unfortunately, the task of the philosophy of nature and of its integrative reflection of scientific descriptions of nature is now neglected by most philosophers. The resulting gap is often filled by natural scientists, who from the perspective of their respective discipline offer generalized philosophical reflections and conjectures concerning the world at large. In this connection, however, the horizon of philosophical problems connected with the respective subject matters and the history of those philosophical problems is not appropriately considered. In these cases it belongs to the task of theology in the dialog with scientists to remind them of the philosophical problems involved in the subject matters dealt with in such dialogs and to argue within such a framework for the specific theological concerns.

The rest of this paper is to exemplify what has been said so far in general terms on the dialog between theology and science in relation to a number of particular issues that appear to me as particularly important for such dialog, because they are important in the foundation of any interpretation of the world. In the first place, some reflections on the concept of law seem to be appropriate, and this in relation to the correlate of law in what is contingently given. The correlation of these two aspects in describing natural processes can be shown in the concept of natural law itself, but this also offers the opportunity for Christian theology to relate the specifically biblical understanding of reality to the description of nature by formulas of law. A second consideration shall focus on the ideas of space and time, which are not only basic in science, but also important in theological affirmations on God's relationship to the world. A third question will deal with the relationship of affirmations about God and about his activity to the movements of bodies, their development and decay—this is the classical theme of scientific descriptions of nature in the framework given by the ideas of space and time. A clarification of how the idea of God relates to space and time, therefore, may have consequences for an understanding of created existence and movement within space and time in their relationship to God. In this connection finally certain conclusions will arise in relation to the concept of evolution, but not only with respect to the evolution of organic life, but also to its setting in the history of the universe.

In 1970 I published an article on "Contingency and Natural Law" that has been the object of close discussion for a number of years in a circle of physicists and theologians and has undergone considerable modifications as a result of these discussions. The subject was interesting from the theological perspective, because the biblical reports on God's action in history emphasize the element of the new and unexpected in divine actions—an emphasis that also characterizes the action of God in the creation of the world. The history of God's action constitutes a unique and irreversible sequence of such contingent acts. The concept of contingency that is used to characterize the divine action in history has its philosophical origin in Aristotle and there it refers to what occurs by chance and to what is non-essential or possible by contrast with the necessary. In Aristotle, however, contingency was connected with the concept of matter, while medieval Christian Aristotelianism, especially since Duns Scot, connected it with God's freedom in his will and action. The concept of natural law, on the other hand, is logically related to conditions of its application that are contingent in relation to the formula of law as such, initial conditions and marginal conditions of the processes described by a formula of law. Those initial and marginal conditions can themselves result from processes that in their turn may be described by formulas of law. This does not change the basic fact, however, that each such description presupposes contingent conditions of its application, with the effect, that the laws of nature may be conceived as descriptions of certain uniformities in natural processes that occur in what basically is contingently given. This implies the assumption that all events are in the first place contingent, even when the sequence of events shows similarities or uniform structures. This consequence appeared to the natural scientists participating in the above mentioned discussions of the sixties as rather problematic, although such an assumption is also suggested by the irreversibility of time. In the meantime, the contingency of events in distinction from contingency in a merely logical sense seems to be generally accepted in view of the fact that many natural processes take place in chaotic forms. Especially, contingency of events can be affirmed with relation to the indeterminacy of elementary events in quantum physics, provided that it is taken into account that the same events, because of the uniformities in their sequence, also become objects of descriptions in terms of natural law. The possibility of such description, on the other hand, does not eliminate the fundamental contingency of events; rather, the regularities that can be observed in contingent sequences of events and can be described by hypotheses of law, are themselves contingent facts. But, while theological affirmations concerning the reality of created existence and the action of God in his creation are primarily related to this aspect of contingency in natural processes, a scientific description of these processes is primarily concerned with the demonstration of regularities in those processes, although the dependence on something contingently given is a precondition in the applicability of the concept of law itself.

To those involved in the sixties in the discussions at Heidelberg a common basis for the dialog between theology and nature seemed to emerge from the clarification of the correlation between natural law and contingency, a common basis beyond vague analogies and metaphors transferred from one discipline to the other. Nevertheless, the agreement on the correlation of natural law and contingency did not yet open an access to a more concrete understanding of nature in theological perspective. In order to find the key to open up such an interpretation, a theological approach to fundamental concepts of physics, like energy or force and movement as well as to their presupposition in ideas about space and time, had to be developed.

In the early eighteenth century a philosophical dispute on the concept of space took place, where theological implications played a decisive role. Even today, the correspondence between Leibniz and Samuel Clarke on Newton's description of space as *sensorium Dei* in his *Optics* 1706, has more than merely historical interest. Certainly, Newton's concept of absolute space has become obsolete to Einstein's theory of relativity, but Newton's thought about space and on God's relation to space was very complex. It is worthwhile to take a closer look to find out just how much of these ideas has become obsolete and what hasn't. The conceptions of absolute direction in space and of absolute dimensions of objects in space are certainly no longer valid. But Newton's and Clarke's ideas about God's relation to space contain another insight that is still important. Clarke defended Newton's attribution of the concept of space to the idea of God against Leibniz' objection that God in such a case would be divisible and composed of parts. Clarke's main argument was that all division in space already presupposes space, because division can only take place within space. The space that is presupposed in all spatial division is infinite and undivided, and this space—not geometrical space that is composed of parts—be identical with the divine immensity that enables God to be present to each of his creatures at their own place. This argument was still reproduced by Kant in his critique of pure reason in 1781—according to Kant the intuition of space as an infinite whole is presupposed in any conception of determinate spaces (A 24f). Kant did no longer explore the theological implications of this idea, because he conceived of space as a merely subjective form of human intuition. As soon as somebody wonders about this subjectivism, however—as it occurred in this century to Samuel Alexander—the theological implications of the priority of infinite and undivided space in relation to every determinate concept of spaces reemerges before one's eyes. The point of this argument is that the infinite space that is presupposed in each division of spaces is necessarily undivided, by contrast to all geometrical conceptions of space. Geometrical concepts of space are constructed on the basis of units of measurement—each geometrical unit of measurement is itself a unit of space the concept of which presupposes the undivided whole of infinite space. That, however, is an infinity that is not to be conceived like it happens in geometry by indefinite addition of units of measurement, but an infinity that is prior to all division and therefore also prior to all forms of measurement. The mistake of Spinoza in his conception of space as an attribute of divine substance consists in the fact that he did not distinguish infinite geometrical space from the infinite and undivided space of the divine immensity that is already presupposed in every geometry. If one considers this distinction, then no pantheistic consequences result from such a close connection between God and space, consequences that Leibniz seems to have suspected in Newton. The transition from the undivided space of divine immensity to the space of our experience that has parts and places can be considered then a consequence of the occurrence of finite objects and their relations to each other. In such a way one can also do justice to the relativity of spatial relations with regard to the masses moving in space. Each type of space that consists of parts presupposes, as Kant emphasized, some undivided whole of space, because divisions and parts are only possible within some space that is already there and therefore prior to geometrical conceptions of space. The ideas about divine immensity and omnipresence with God's creatures can be referred to this presupposition of undivided space, like Newton and Clarke did, without violating the divine transcendence over the world, in contrast to the conception of Spinoza that Einstein felt sympathetic with, which however, did not distinguish between the undivided infinite space of divine omnipresence and the space of geometry.

The relationship between God's eternity and time is largely analogous to that between his immensity and space. Kant's treatment of time in his transcendental aesthetics corresponded closely to this treatment of the idea of space—in both cases an infinite and undivided whole is considered the precondition of all division and of all conceptions of parts. With reference to time this means—"Different times are but parts of one and the same time" (A31). The undivided whole of time or rather the whole of life that appears divided in the sequence of time, has been termed eternity in the philosophical and theological tradition since Plotinus' treatise on time in his *Enneads*. Eternity, Plotinus says, is ultimate completion without parts or division (III, 7, 11) of what occurs in divided form in the sequence of time. Boethius, who transmitted this definition to later generations, called eternity the simultaneous and complete presence of unlimited life (*interminabilis vitae tota simul et perfecta possessio*, De Cons. phil. V, 6, 4). Eternity, then, is not atemporal in the sense that eternity and time were completely foreign to each other. Rather, according to Plotinus, time is constituted by eternity, because the transition from one temporal moment to the next is understandable only if we presuppose some presence of the whole that is separated in the sequence of temporal moments even within that separation, in other words, a presence of eternity in the course of time itself. The same idea is expressed in Kant's sentence, different times are just parts of one and the same time. But Kant did no longer see time as constituted by the presence of eternity, but in analogy to his conception of space he thought time constituted on the subject of experience, more precisely on the "standing and persisting" human ego (A 123) which, as persisting through time, according to Kant, forms the basis of the unity of all human experience. In view of the temporality of the ego itself, however, that we are aware of in our self-consciousness, Kant's attempt of accounting for the unity of time on the basis of the unity of the subject may seem to be considerably more problematic than Plotinus' foundation of time on the concept of eternity.

From a theological perspective of nature, then, God's eternity is present in time, more specifically as origin and completion of time and of all temporal reality—origin in the sense of conditioning the continuity of what occurs separately in the sequence of time, completion, however, because all temporal reality according to Plotinus tends toward the future in order to realize the whole of its being. It is through the future that eternity enters into time.

With relation to time as well as to space, the result is that these ideas cannot be successfully defined on the basis of measurement by clocks or by spatial units of measurement. This may be a very important point in the dialog between theology and science, because the scientific interest in time, as well as in spatial dimensions, is so closely connected with the possibility of measurement. The ideas of space and time, however, claim priority with relation to all techniques of measurement. If this priority is neglected, contradictions are the inevitable consequence. This is so because all units of measurement are themselves already parts of time and space, that have to be delimited within time and space from other such parts and therefore already presuppose time and space as such.

Much more difficult than the question of the relationship of space and time to God's immensity and eternity is a clarification of God's relation to the forces working in the movements of nature. And yet this is a decisive question for every biblically-based doctrine on creation, because at this point the possibility of an action of God in His creation is at stake, an action not only in the beginning, but also in the entire process of the history of His creation. It was at this point that in the seventeenth and eighteenth centuries the alienation between Christian theology and the scientific description of nature began. The starting point of this alienation was the mechanistic interpretation of natural processes that Descartes already had inaugurated and that against Newton's intentions triumphed in the eighteenth century, when all natural force was reduced to bodies and to their effects upon each other. This conception necessarily excluded God from the understanding of natural processes. If there was a point, where modern philosophical theology was in unanimous agreement with the earlier scholastic teaching about God, it was the affirmation that God cannot be a body. Consequently any idea of an exercise of power issuing from God and consequently any assumption of divine action in the course of nature was apriori excluded, if all natural force resides in bodies. Thus God was respectfully urged out of the natural world.

When the far-reaching consequences of the reduction of the forces of natural movements to conceptions of bodies and masses toward producing an atheistic picture of nature are duly considered, one also can imagine the potential significance of the introduction of field concepts into the description of natural processes since Faraday in favor of a theological interpretation of natural processes. This statement does not mean that the demonstration of the efficacy of electric and magnetic fields could immediately be used as a model to conceive of God's efficacy in nature. But although field effects usually have their correlate in masses, Faraday already entertained a vision of finally interpreting all bodily phenomena as manifestations of fields. A vision like that was close to that of Newton that the forces of natural movement are finally not material, they do not issue from bodies. Rather, Newton conceived of God's efficacy in the universe in analogy to how our spirit moves the parts of our body.

An introduction of the field concept into theology is not, however, primarily suggested by the question of how to understand God's activity in nature, but it is suggested first by internal problems in the doctrine of God. The designation of the divine being as "spirit" in the Gospel of John (John 4:24) has been interpreted since Origin in the sense that God is *Nus,* a bodiless spiritual intellect, but this platonizing interpretation does not correspond to the original meaning of this biblical word *pneuma* nor to the corresponding Hebrew word *ruach.* In both cases the root meaning is moved air, breath, even wind. In Greek thought the word *pneuma,* which is usually translated by "spirit," was used in the sense of air in movement like in breath or wind. This applies to the presocratic philosophers, especially to Anaximenes, but also and particularly to the Stoics. According to Stoic doctrine, air as the most subtle element penetrates everything and keeps together the entire cosmos through its particular "tension" (*tónos*). The early Christian theologians before the third century understood the New Testament identification of God as *pneuma* in similar ways. Now one of the most renowned historians of science in our century, Max Jammer, who investigated the history of a number of key concepts of physics, considers the *pneuma* concepts of classical antiquity as predecessors of the field concepts of modern physics. Indeed, the intuitive idea of a field of power comes to paradigmatic expression in a state of tension in the air. Modern field concepts, however, differ in an important point from the conceptions of *pneuma* in classical antiquity—field effects do not require, although in the nineteenth century this was still assumed, a material medium like air or "ether." They can pervade space without such a medium. The materialism of the Stoic doctrine of *pneuma* as air, however, in the sense of a most subtle element that penetrates everything else, formed the main reason of Origen's rejection of this conception in interpreting the Johannine characterizing of God as spirit. The absurdities of a conception of God as body—divisible and composed of parts—formed the negative reason for interpreting *pneuma* in terms of *Nus,* and thus for conceiving of God in the image of a bodiless intellect. Now it is evident that this conception does not correspond to the root meaning of *pneuma*. At this point the field concept that replaces the *pneuma* doctrines of classical antiquity can become helpful in theology, because it allows to distinguish the root meaning of *pneuma* from the conception of a material basis or medium. If the divine reality is conceived in terms of a field that manifests itself in the three "persons" of Father, Son, and Holy Spirit, then one can do justice to Origen's objections against any conception of God as body and yet preserve the genuine meaning of *pneuma*.

Is such a theological use of the field concept a mere metaphor? At the first moment it may look like that. But one should not overlook that the fundamental requirement for the application of the concept of field is met in theology. That is the relationship to time and space, though in the sense of what has been said about the undivided infinite space of divine immensity, presupposed in all geometrical description of space, and about the undivided unity of time in God's eternity as condition of all temporal sequence. The interpretation of the pneumatic particularity of God's being as field, can be accounted for by relating it to the undivided wholeness of time and space prior to all geometrical description. By the same reason it is distinguished from the field concepts of physics, but would function as a condition of those in analogy to what had to be said concerning space and time. The field of divine omnipotence, then, does not compete with concrete physical fields, but its activity works through all the natural forces without being exhausted by them. Like God's omnipresence is copresent to all things without falling prey to the relativistic paradoxes of simultaneity, since God's omnipresence is not dependent on the velocity of light, in a similar way the field effects the divine omnipresence are not in need of being transmitted by waves. The concept of waves, though important in the field notions of classical physics and especially as a basis of quantitative description of field effects may not be constitutive of the field concept as such, while that concept would be empty with being related to time and space. If the concept of field in the strict sense can be conceived of without the idea of expanding through waves, then also types of non-local, instantaneous communication between physical phenomena can be conceived of in terms of field effects.

In the framework of this paper it is no longer possible to apply what has been said so far upon a theological interpretation of the world of creatures according to the sequence of their emergence in the history of the universe. A sketch of such an interpretation has been published in the context of my treatment of the doctrine of creation in the second volume of my *Systematic Theology*. In the dialog between theology and science, however, it is still more important to reach agreement about the foundations of interpretations of such a type. Only this much may be said here—the key for perceiving the interconnection of eternity and time lies with the relevance of the future in understanding everything existing in time. It is through the future that eternity enters into time. Ever new contingent events proceed from the future, and on the other hand everything existing in time can expect from the future only the possible wholeness of its life. All things proceed towards the kingdom of God, but God's sovereignty is already at work by entering from His future into the presence of His creatures. From the point of view of the creatures this relationship gets reverted. The future becomes the direction of extrapolations from the present and from whatever we know from the past. That is also true in the history of the universe. Mythical interpretation of the world looks at the order of the universe as founded in its beginning. Even the biblical report on creation, though no longer a myth in its literal form, exemplifies this way of looking at the world. The image of the foundation of all creaturely forms, in a first week of seven days, is in a certain tension, however, to the perspective otherwise characteristic for the biblical understanding of reality, the perspective of ever new actions of God in the history toward the future completion of His creation. The idea of an order of creation, complete in the beginning and not significantly changed in subsequent time made an agreement between theologians and scientists difficult for a long period, especially during the struggle about the doctrine of evolution. Much more important, however, in view of a possible consonance between a theology of creation and natural science, is that the evolution of life occurs within an irreversible process, where again and again contingencies occur. It is similar with the history of the universe. With regard to the origin and evolution of life as well as in the field of cosmology the ideological barriers between the scientific description of the world and the interpretation of the same world in Christian theology broke down. One would ask too much, if scientific cosmology were expected to produce right away a demonstration of the existence of God, as Pope Pius XII believed at the time of the first enthusiasm about the present standard model of the expanding universe. It is sufficient that theological interpretation of the history of the universe in terms of creation can be developed in consonance with scientific data and procedures. To this end it is necessary that the theological doctrine of creation remains able to learn, not in the sense of adapting itself apologetically to every change of the scientific description of nature, but in the sense that theology remains vigorous enough to develop from its own resources ever new interpretations that try to do justice to a changing state of experiential knowledge of our world, in order to integrate it into the Christian understanding of the world as being created by the God of the Bible.

# THE EMERGENCE OF CREATURES AND THEIR SUCCESSION IN A DEVELOPING UNIVERSE

WOLFHART PANNENBERG

I

The term "create" serves in the biblical tradition and in Christian theology to relate the reality of the world to the God of the Jews. It expresses a rather specific way of conceiving the divine origin of the world. The term "create" emphasizes the unconditional and free character of the divine act of producing the world and thus it indicates the contingency of the world itself and of each part of it as well as of the divine act and puts it into being.

This way of accounting for the reality of the world seems to have emerged in the sixth century before Christ, at the time of the Babylonian exile of the intellectual leadership of the Jewish people. The priestly document on the creation of the world by the God of Israel, now the first chapter of the Bible, answered the challenge of the Babylonian religion, especially the description of the way the world was built in the *enuma elish*. The priestly text says that it was not Marduk, but the God of Israel who produced the universe and that He did it in the characteristic way of His action according to how the prophetic tradition had described God's action in history—with sovereign freedom, unconditioned by any other factor than God Himself.

The account given in this text is significantly different from the older narrative on the creation of human beings and of the world surrounding them. The narrative in the second chapter of our Bible focuses almost exclusively on Adam and Eve, while the priestly report in the first chapter intends to comprise the entire universe and carefully attributes to each part its proper place. This indicates the doctrinal character of the priestly texts that distinguishes it from the earlier narrative, where even the very term "create" was not yet used. The difference is explained by the fact that the priestly document responds to the challenge of the Babylonian epic by claiming the world in all its parts for the God of Israel to whose creative activity each part of it owes its existence.

The apologetic and doctrinal intention of the priestly report on the creation of the universe was executed by seizing upon elements from the Babylonian and other mythological descriptions of the origin of the world as well as upon materials from wisdom traditions, especially from their efforts at collecting the different forms of natural phenomena and arranging them in catalogues. Regarding both types of materials one is entitled to judge that the priestly document made comprehensive use of the science of its day in critically selecting and interpreting its results by relating them to the creative activity of God. Whatever was known at that time about the natural world and the different forms of creatures was incorporated in the priestly document. In combining the wisdom materials with the mythological quest for the origin of the universe, the priestly document certainly claimed to provide true explanation of the existence of the different forms of reality. And it did so in a remarkably sober, occasionally almost rationalistic way. The description in Gen. 1:6-9 of how God made a divide in the primeval water to separate what was beneath the divide from further supply of water from above with the natural consequence that the waters beneath the divide would recede and let the dry ground emerge is a beautiful example of ancient engineering and thoroughly rationalistic. Such rationalism fits very well with the monotheistic emphasis that puts all the stress on the divine command as cause of the emergence of new forms of reality.

## II

The priestly report on the origin of the universe from a creative action of the God of Israel is a document from an ancient culture, and nobody should expect that the assertions of such a document could agree in all details with our contemporary scientific knowledge on the origin and development of the universe. In fact, given the historical distance, one should expect that our present conception of the universe of nature and of its history would have less in common with such an ancient document than is actually the case. There is rough agreement, first, concerning the fact that our universe had a beginning and that it developed along a succession of stages or steps, however those steps are conceived materially. But also concerning the material content of those steps and of their sequence, more similarity is to be observed than one might expect—light at the beginning of the series, human beings at its end, the priority of light over the formation of stars, including sun and moon, furthermore the production of plants by the earth, the function of vegetation as a presupposition of animal life, the close relationship between human beings and mammals, called "animals of the land" in the priestly creation report (Gen. 1:24-25). Both kinds of creature appear, according to the biblical report, in the sixth day of creation in distinction from the animals of the water and from the birds.

Such similarities, of course, are limited by dissimilarities—the creation of the earth separated in the biblical report from the formation of the stars and prior to them. This is due to the utilitarian perspective of the priestly report in dealing with the stars and especially with the sun and moon. There is an unmistakable demythologizing bias effective at this point, because in Babylon like in other ancient cultures the stars were closely connected with deities. Therefore, their importance had to be reduced in this Jewish account on the origin of the universe. The example shows, however, how religious prejudices occasionally distort the presentation of natural facts.

Other limitations in the biblical report are simply due to limitations of knowledge as it was available at the time. Thus the concept of life is limited to animals (Gen. 1:30), to the exclusion of plants, and the classification of animals according to the places of their life differs from later classifications according to families and species. There are other, more important differences between the biblical report on the creation of the universe and the modern understanding of its origin and development. But before turning to them, it seems appropriate to engage in some more general and more fundamental reflection on the question of where the authority resides that this text enjoys in Christian teaching.

III

For many centuries, a literal authority was ascribed to the biblical report on the creation of the world as part of the inspired word of the divine Scripture. Even today this view continues with many Christians who are afraid that the authority of Scripture disintegrates as soon as one admits any incorrectness in detail. The consequence of such a fundamentalistic view of the authority of Scripture is that one has to cling to the infallible truth of every single proposition in the text. There is no room, then, for appreciating the priestly report on creation as a document from an ancient culture, sharing the achievements, but also the limitations, of its cultural setting. Such an attitude, however, amounts to an obliteration of the authentic character of the biblical text itself. It is precisely in its form as a document of an ancient culture that the authority of the text must reside. This also applies to the report on the creation of the universe. If that is so, the authority of the text cannot coincide with the infallible truth of its particular sentences, as if they were superior to all later experience. Neither can the authority of such a text consist in the old-fashioned view of a past stage in the development of human culture. This last statement, however, is somewhat dangerous, for everything in such a text can easily be denounced as belonging to a past cultural situation and can therefore be dismissed as no longer relevant. On the line of such a way of arguing any authority of the cultural tradition can be denied, and yet in human cultural history there is, sometimes at least, authority of the content of the cultural tradition in spite of cultural changes. Therefore, it is always necessary to distinguish between elements that have become obsolete and others that are still valid. What, then, is at the basis of the continuing authority of a key document of our cultural tradition like the biblical report on the creation of the universe?

Christians will argue that at the basis of such continuing authority there is the continuing faith in the God of Israel and of Jesus Christ. Then the authority of the biblical report on creation must be looked for not in particular propositions, but in the way it gives witness to the divine reality of the God of the Bible. This was done, as I said earlier, by affirming the universe to exist as a result of the creative action of the God of Israel. The priestly document made this affirmation in the form of a detailed account of how the universe came into being. To this purpose it made use of all the material knowledge about the world that was at its disposal. In this act, then, of claiming the universe with all its content to exist as God's creation, resides the authority of the biblical report. That authority is obeyed not when the individual statements of that ancient text are preserved and repeated, but when the act of laying claim on the universe to exist as consequence of God's creative action is repeated, and it has to be repeated by using the material knowledge of one's own time about the world in similarity to the paradigmatic biblical teaching on creation. In the modern situation, it is necessary to that purpose to use the resources of modern science rather than to cling to the individual statements of the text against the empirical evidence of modern science.

But how can theology let itself be guided by the paradigm of the biblical report in getting involved in the scientific materials of a later period? The task is facilitated by the observation of basic similarities between the biblical approach and our modern view of the origin and development of the natural universe. The basic similarity consists in looking at the universe in terms of a sequence of emergent new forms, and in the framework of that overall similarity we may try to deal with the more profound dissimilarities and differences.

## IV

In the judgment of my teacher Edmund Schlink, the deepest difference between the modern view of nature and the biblical report consists in the modern conception that new forms of reality emerge from the autonomous activity of nature itself, while according to the biblical view the creatures enjoy their autonomous activity only within the limits of a divine order of their existence that was put up in the beginning.

This judgment contains obvious elements of truth. Thus the different genera and species of vegetation and animal life were put up, according to the priestly report, in the beginning by the creator and remain unchanged. He granted to plants and animals the power of propagation, but such power of propagation only serves to perpetuate the character of the species. It doesn't change the nature of species as it would correspond to the modern view of natural evolution. At this point the contrast is perfectly clear.

But on the other hand, the creative activity of God can very well be effective, according to the biblical report, through the medium of a created reality. Thus, in Gen. 1:11 God addresses the earth to produce vegetation, and the earth is called upon once more in Gen. 1:24 to bring forth the animals living on it. Herein, even animal life is understood to be a product of the earth. The biblical creation story does not exclude, then, mediating agencies in the act of God's creation. In this respect, there is no opposition between the biblical report and the basic intuition of the modern idea of natural evolution. So far the difference is mainly that in modern theory the productivity of the earth is replaced by the idea of nature and, when it comes to the origin of life, by the idea of a self-organization of matter and of the creative evolution of life itself.

The difficulty in comparing the biblical report and the modern conception of organic evolution resides at a different point, in the conception of the priestly document, of course, that the act of creation was completed at the end of a first period of the world's existence, while in the modern view the evolution of life and the universe continues through the entire duration of the world's existence.

At this point, however, the priestly report on the creation of the universe is not typical of all forms of the biblical witness. In Psalm 104 we have an account of God's creative activity that describes it in terms of a continuing source of the existence of the creatures (esp. Ps. 104:30). Similarly, in second Isaiah God's action in history is presented as a creative activity in the sense of bringing forth something new and formerly unknown (Isa. 43:19), and in expressing this idea the prophet uses the same terminology (*bara*) that functions in the priestly document as a technical term referring to the creation in the beginning. The idea of a continuing creative activity of God, then, is not foreign to the biblical witness, though of course not combined with the idea of evolution as in our modern view. It is the continuing creation of something new, on which the existence of the creatures depends. That idea differs from the traditional dogmatic term *creatio continua* which meant only the preservation of what had been created before. In view of second Isaiah, it is the production of new things that continues. The intention of the priestly document in Genesis 1 to limit the notion of creation to God's activity in the beginning, is only one variation of expressing the biblical faith in God's creative activity as the source of everything.

What was the motivation behind this particular variation in the conception of God's creative activity? One may distinguish two factors here, one more mythological and a more theological concern of lasting importance. The theological concern was for the stability and reliability of the order of creation. In view of the priestly document, such stability depends on the unchanged form of things as they were established in the beginning. The modern understanding of nature is also interested in that element of stability. But we see the stability of nature warranted by the invariable validity of the laws that govern natural processes. Thus one can argue that this concern of the biblical report has been satisfied in the modern conception of nature, though in a different way.

The mythological motivation in the priestly report on the creation of the world is to be found in its function to legitimate the Jewish week of seven days and in particular the institution of the sabbath at its end. On the basis of the priestly document the Jewish week, with the sabbath at its end, is seen as indefinitely repeating the original week of God's work of creation with the seventh day of rest at its end. Accordingly, in the decalogue of Exodus 20 the commandment to observe the sabbath day is based on the order of creation: "for in six days the Lord made heaven and earth, and all that is in them, and rested the seventh day; therefore the Lord blessed the sabbath day and hallowed it" (Exod. 20:11).

Interestingly enough, in early Jewish exegesis the seven days of creation could be interpreted differently by relating the sequence of seven days to the entire history of the world rather than confining it to an original period. In the Jewish apocalyptic literature (esp. Enoch 91 and 93), the seventh day was understood to refer to the future consummation of the world in the kingdom of God, and in Hebrews 4 the Christian hope for the eschatological future of God was described as a hope to enter into God's own rest after the labor of creation. In Enoch 71:15, the seventh day of God's rest, identified with the future aeon of consummation, was even described as the source from which peace is pouring since the first creation of the world. The peace of the sabbath, then, could be understood as an anticipation of the final piece in the kingdom of God. The interpretations of the week of creation are interesting in the context of the present argument, because in their own way they combine the image of an original period of creation with the idea of a creative activity of God continuing through the history of the world until its consummation in the eschatological future of God's kingdom. One must not mistake, however, this view for being the view of the priestly report on the creation of the world and the first chapter of the Bible. There the act of creation is limited to a first period in the history of the world.

## V

Important as the difference is between the idea of a creation of the universe in an initial period of the world's history and the conception of a continuing creative activity of God corresponding to the creative development of the natural world, still this is not the most profound difference between our modern understanding of natural processes and biblical view. The deepest difference, rather, is connected with the *atomistic* perspective of modern science according to which all natural forms are composed of more elementary particles and processes. This perspective originated from a particular form of ancient Greek philosophy of nature, from Democritos, and it influenced modern science to such an extend that the development and sequence of natural forms in the history of nature are no longer conceivable without it, though the search for the final elements of matter led to more complicated results than they could have been expected on the basis of Democritos' atomic theory. Most importantly, there is not just one type of elementary particles, but several. Furthermore, the difference between particles and events is vanishing, when so-called particles have no more than momentary existence. Nevertheless, the idea that the qualitative differences of natural forms can be reduced to different combinations of elementary particles has been victorious.

Accordingly, in the perspective of modern science, the sequence of natural forms starts with elementary phenomena out of which all more complex forms of reality developed. This perspective is significantly different from the biblical report on the creation of the universe, but it does not necessarily contradict its theological intention. The atomistic view of the universe and of its development has often been perceived as an alternative to a theology of creation, and this would be the case if it rendered God superfluous in understanding the reality of nature. Such could be a consequence of reducing all natural phenomena to combinations of elementary units, if that meant that the elementary units are finally the only factors in explaining natural processes and the emergence of natural forms. In fact, however, the interaction and combination of elementary units that is involved in the emergence of more complex forms seems to always require conditions of a holistic nature forming the context of elementary processes. As early as 1966 Ian Barbour called on de Broglie and on the Pauli Exclusion Principle as expressing the underivable function of the whole in conditioning the parts. A whole either in the form of environment or field or as manifest in a system of higher order like the atom in relation to subatomic particles provides the context for the more elementary processes taking place within it.

In the case of the early universe, the state of that universe as a whole must have functioned as the comprehensive condition of the elementary processes going on within it. They took place under the conditions of such high temperatures that the state of the universe did not allow for the formation of more complex and enduring forms of reality. It needed the expansion of the universe and the concomitant process of cooling down to develop conditions that allow for the formation of atoms and molecules and furthermore, under the influence of gravity, for their conglomeration to galaxies and stars. Thus, in a modern view, the development of the universe is also a development of complex and enduring forms out of elementary processes. But it is also true that the changing stay of the universe imposes conditions on the continuous functioning of those processes.

The importance of a holistic framework in the emergence of new forms of existence has also been pointed out with relation to the formation of a biosphere on our earth—the spontaneous emergence of life depends on a complicated texture of very special conditions as they develop on this particular planet. Life itself seems now to have emerged through spontaneous self-organization, once those conditions were given and a thermodynamic gradient could be exploited like in the case of the flame that nourishes its life from the potential energy of the candle. Long before the mechanism of life, its dissipative nature, was understood, the flame of a candle was considered a symbol of life in its effort at temporarily preserving its form at the price of consuming the energies of its environment.

As the emergence of living organisms is conditioned by the formation of a biosphere on our earth, while this in turn is conditioned by the particular state of the expanding universe, the universe as a whole seems arranged in such a way as to make organic life possible. This is the basic idea that recently has been discussed under the name of "anthropic principle." It means that the emergence of organic life and finally of human beings is not an insignificant accident of nature as compared to the vastness of the universe. This had been the feeling of sensitive thinkers like Pascal in early modernity, by contrast to the biblical view of the creation of the world, where the entire sequence of creatures led up to the creation of human beings. The feeling of being at a loss in the vast spaces of the universe is no longer assumed to contemporary scientific cosmology. The natural constants of the universe are arranged in such a way as to make organic life and intelligent animals like ourselves possible. I do not want to go beyond this "weak" form of the anthropic principle by claiming that the emergence of intelligent life be *necessary* on the basis of how the order of the universe is arranged from its beginnings. I am quite satisfied with the contingent nature of the emergence of life as well as of other natural forms in the history of the universe. But the emergence of life and of intelligent life, as in human beings, is no longer to be considered an insignificant accident in the history of the universe.

## VI

Some such view of the universe as a totality that conditions the particular processes going on within it and the emergence of ever more complex forms of enduring existence seems to be required in a theological interpretation of nature in terms of creation. A conception of the universe as an ordered system corresponds to the unity of the one God who is supposed to be its creator, and the place of particular phenomena within that systematic order as well as in relation to its divine origin determines their individual significance. On the other hand, contingency of events in general and of the emergence of new forms of reality in particular prevents the individual forms and processes from becoming completely dependent on the systematic whole of the universe and preserves an element of immediacy in them with relation to their ultimate origin. Such contingency of natural phenomena, however, seems bound up with their temporal nature, if time is to be conceived as an irreversible flux of events, where each event is finally unique and the future always bringing about something new, notwithstanding all the regularities applying in the sequence of events.

These requirements of a theological interpretation of nature in terms of creation are met in the biblical creation report—the universe is ordered in a sequence of six days of God's work, and the significance of each work of creation is given by its place in that sequence and in the relations to other creatures such place entails. Each new work, however, is presented as contingent with regard to what went before, and that is expressed by the origin of each new work of creation in the divine word of command. Finally, the elements of systematic order and of contingency in detail are combined in the scheme of a temporal series in the emergence of the creatures.

The abiding importance of the biblical creation report may very well be perceived then in the fact that it stands as a paradigmatic exemplification of a systematic scheme which meets these three requirements of an overall systematic order, of contingency in detail and of temporal sequence in the emergence of particular forms. Each new theological doctrine of creation that will integrate theologically the scientific knowledge of its time has to meet these same requirements in order to give a theological account of the world of nature as God's creation. Such an interpretation is not superfluous with regard to our experiential knowledge about nature and it is not an arbitrary imposition upon a scientific cosmology. At present I want to emphasize that as compared with those three requirements of a theological interpretation of nature it is of secondary importance, whether organic life made its appearance on earth as completely new phenomenon or whether it emerged in a process of spontaneous self-organization from inorganic matter, and it is also of secondary importance, whether or not each new species is to be considered as a discontinuous new beginning or as a product of the continuous process of organic evolution of life. Also of secondary importance, finally, is the question of whether or not the emergence of human beings derived from the development of organic species rather than coming into existence without mediation by other creatures. I mentioned earlier that even in the biblical report such mediating function of a creature in producing new forms of existence was not considered to be opposed to the origin of the new creature from a divine act of creation, as the function ascribed to the earth in producing vegetation and animals demonstrates. Important in a theological interpretation of nature is that each new form of existence is recognized as contingent fact and hence as immediate to the ultimate cause of all. This immediacy to the ultimate cause of all, however, is itself conditioned by the place of the new creature in the sequence of others, because the divine act of creation relates to each individual creature in the context of the universe God created and not an abstraction from everything else. In this way even the emergence of human beings is seen in the biblical creation report as conditioned by the preceding stages of created existence and related to them.

In a modern perspective, then, the expansion of the universe might be perceived as the instrument of the creator in producing enduring and independent forms of created existence. The expansion of the universe does not only provide space for a multitude of creatures, but more importantly the concomitant cooling effect provides the basic condition for all forms of higher organization, higher complexity, beginning with the formation of atoms and molecules. Organic life emerged as a still higher form of such complexity and, at the same time, of independent existence. Though organisms are less durable than atoms and stars, the self-organization of life expresses an element of spontaneity which constitutes a higher form of independent existence. In the biblical report this was expressed by the idea that living creatures are distinguished from others by sharing an apportion of the divine Spirit, the cause of life. In modern times a similar idea has been expressed by Teilhard de Cardin by the affirmation that on the higher levels of complexity there are also increasing degrees of interiority of existence.

Human beings emerged at the end of this sequence, as far as our knowledge goes. In the biblical creation report this place of humanity implies a special relationship to the rest of creation on the one hand, to the creator of all on the other. And here we arrive at a further distinguishing characteristic of a theological interpretation of nature as creation of God—of the biblical God—and therefore in a Jewish or Christian interpretation of nature. In distinction from other religious traditions, the biblical view of humanity's place in creation is certainly anthropocentric, and the Christian doctrine of God's incarnation in one human person and by that person in humanity puts a particular and ultimate emphasis on that anthropocentric position. But it is not a narrow type of anthropocentrism that would shut itself off from anything else. It is an inclusive anthropocentrism that relates the human predicament of the destiny of the entire universe in the light of its divine origin. It is a form of anthropocentrism, therefore, that involves a responsibility of humanity for other creatures as far as the range of human activity extends. When in the biblical report the human beings are commissioned to exercise dominion over the earth and everything on it, that does not mean that all other creatures are delivered to arbitrary disposal according to human license, but the divine commission aims at a form of dominion that represents within the created universe the authority of the creator Himself and therefore involves responsibility for attending to God's creation and to His resolution of granting some degree of independent existence to the products of His creative activity. The place of the human being at the point of culmination of God's creation inevitably involves that kind of responsibility in correlation with the special relationship of that creature to God the creator of all.

# CHRISTIANITY AND
# SECULARISM

WOLFHART PANNENBERG

I

In the course of this century the cultural context of Christian churches changed significantly. The culture became more visibly non-religious than it had been before. Certainly, the separation between church and state originated two centuries earlier. But that did not necessarily entail an alienation of the culture from its religious roots. With the exception of Judaism, most of the different churches that came to enjoy unrestricted activities after the abolishment of an established religion, were Christian denominations so that the predominately Christian, even Protestant character of the American culture was not deeply changed as an immediate consequence of the separation between church and state. In other Western societies more explicit links with some or another Christian church continued to be effective until the present century. Nevertheless, it will become evident that the roots of the process of secularization that resulted in the present alienation of the public culture from religion and especially from Christianity, can be traced back to the seventeenth century.

In the contemporary situation, the climate of secularism puts considerable strain on the confidence of believers in the truth of the Christian teaching. It is the situation Peter L. Berger described years ago in his book *A Rumor of Angels* (1969), in terms of the situation of a cognitive minority whose standards of knowledge deviate from those that are publicly taken for granted. Plausibility, Berger wrote, "in the sense of what people actually find credible, of views of reality depends upon the social support these receive." Where this social plausibility weakens, it requires additional personal strength to maintain beliefs that are no longer in line with those dominant in the social context. This is a social and psychological situation that has nothing to do with the question of truth. "It is, of course," says Berger, "possible to go against the social consensus that sur-

rounds us, but there are powerful pressures [which manifest themselves as psychological pressures within our own consciousness] to conform to the views and beliefs of
our fellow men"(43). This is precisely the strain which the secularist culture puts on
the consciousness and behavior of Christians in Western societies that were formerly
more or less strongly influenced by Christian values and beliefs.

One consequence of the secularist mood is that the extent of sheer knowledge
about Christian teachings, biblical names and events, and the history of Christianity is
dwindling. The situation is no longer that some people reject the truth claims of
Christian teachings. Increasing numbers of them don't even know about what should
be accepted or rejected. This is remarkable because Christianity has been so important in our cultural tradition. One cannot understand Western culture and its history
without the Christian religion. The more widespread the lack of information about
the contents of the Bible and Christian teachings, however, the easier the creeping up
of prejudices against Christianity, especially the prejudice that Christianity has been
an oppressive form of religion. Therefore, even when people are getting interested in
religion again, which is a natural reaction against the lack of deeper meaning in the
secularist culture, they would not normally turn to Christianity, but rather to alternative forms of religion.

The difficulties of the Christian message in this cultural situation have been sharp-
ened recently by tendencies to relativize the concern for truth. While the enlightenment challenged the traditional Christian affirmations by demanding rational argument for the truth claims of Christian teaching instead of a simple appeal to authority,
now truth claims as such are considered obsolete. This turns Christian doctrines into
mere opinions that may be affirmed or not according to individual options and prefer-
ence. The dissolution of the notion of truth, however, ruins the idea of Christian missions. Missionary preaching is no longer seen as bringing the truth to other people—
and therefore legitimate—but as imposing upon them one's personal opinions, which
must appear improper. And even when we leave the issue of missions aside, why
should people opt for the Christian faith, if not because the apostolic teaching is true?
Or, more precisely, if it is not even meaningful to claim its content to be true? The
issue of truth is absolutely vital for the Christian faith. The destruction of the idea of
truth, on the other hand, can be seen as a strategy of legitimating the secularist culture
since its lack of true meaning is precisely the point of its most delicate vulnerability.

## II

Secularism and even modern culture in general have sometimes been characterized
as a phenomenon of apostasy from the Christian faith. The most important Christian
thinker who took that view was Karl Barth. In Karl Barth's opinion, modern culture
has been a revolt against the Christian faith in putting the human being in the place
of God. There is much that can be said in favor of such an interpretation of modern
culture. The concept of human nature has indeed become basic in modern culture in
a way that can be compared to the religious foundation of the cultural system in earlier periods of history. The concern for human rights is but one aspect, though politically the most important aspect of the occupation of modern culture with human

nature and whatever belongs to it. Increasingly that meant to make the human individual the highest value and criterion. But does that modern tendency possess no truth whatsoever in a Christian view? Should it simply be rejected as modern apostasy? Is not the emphasis on the individual person of distinctively Christian origin? Does not Christianity have a great deal in common with that modern spirit? Did it not even contribute to liberate the Christian consciousness itself from the distortion of intolerance? The relationship between the Christian faith and modernity seems more ambivalent than to allow for a simple rejection of modernity by Christians. Though modern culture, in turning secularist, contributed to the alienation of a great many people from the Christian faith, it is still necessary for Christians to learn and remember the lesson that the rise of modernity teaches and to appropriate its positive values to the Christian consciousness itself.

## III

The distinction between the secular and the religious or spiritual realm had a long history in the development of Christianity. In earlier centuries that distinction did not imply the complete separation and emancipation of the secular segments of social life—the political and economic system, but also law and parts of the educational system and arts—from the spiritual life of the church. To the contrary, the distinction between the secular and the religious sphere had itself a Christian basis. The Christian awareness that the present order of society is not yet the kingdom of God, but an imperfect and provisional form of social life, lies at the root of the distinction between the secular and the spiritual. It is a distinction that sets Christianity apart from other religiously imbued cultures like Islam. It separated the Byzantinian Empire already from the pre-Christian Roman empire, because in the post-Constantinian period there was a balance between the authority of the bishops and that of the emperor, while in Ancient Rome the emperor himself had been the highest priest, *pontifex maximus*.

The distinction between the religious and the secular, however, took on another significance after the Reformation of the sixteenth century or, more precisely, after the century of religious wars that followed in the wake of the breakup of the medieval church which had been the unwanted result of the Reformation. When in a number of European countries no religious party could get the upper hand in the attempt of imposing its own faith upon the entire society, the unity of the social system had to be based on a foundation other than religion, since religion had proved to disrupt the social peace. In the second half of the seventeenth century, therefore, most people became convinced that religious controversies had to be bracketed if social peace was to be restored. This was the historical movement when modern secular culture was born.

In earlier centuries, such a step would have been unimaginable. Even in the century of the Reformation, religious unity was generally considered indispensable for the unity of a society. This was the reason why neither Luther nor Calvin could conceive the possibility of religious toleration, though they emphasized the decisive importance of the individual conscience in matters of religious faith. The step toward religious freedom and toleration was first taken in the Netherlands, near the end of the sixteenth century, in order to restore peace between the Catholic and Protestant parts of the population of that country. The principle of religious freedom and toleration was proclaimed by William of Orange with the confidence of acting in line with the Protestant understanding of the Christian faith, in line with the liberty of a Christian, which Luther had thought and with the appeal to conscience in matters of faith. But actually it was a significant step towards a complete reconstruction of the social system and of the culture itself.

The older assumption that the unity of society requires unity of religious faith at its basis was not without good reasons. If the citizens are to obey the law and the authority of a civil government, they must believe that it is right to do so and that they do not simply succumb to the caprice of those in power. To this end the wielding of power must be regarded legitimate in the name of some authority beyond human arbitrariness and manipulation. In other words, religion must oblige and restrain those in power as well as those upon whom such power is exercised. In such cases the subjects can feel united with those entrusted with legislative and administrative power in common responsibility to some authority that stands above all of them. If there is no religious unity, however, the legitimacy of government is jeopardized and so is social peace among its subjects.

Such reasoning seems long obsolete. But it has never been effectively refuted. It was dismissed for pragmatic reasons, because of the urgent need to restore social peace in spite of religious differences and controversies. Alternative legitimations of government were developed, of course, replacing the religious one. Most important of these alternative legitimations became the idea of representative government. But still the plausibility of such legitimation is more pragmatic than theoretically secure.

## IV

So far I suggested that the origin of modern secular culture is to be looked for at the end of the period of religious wars in post-Reformation Europe, generally in the second half of the seventeenth century, though earlier in the case of the Netherlands. In order to restore social peace in multi-confessional societies, the political system, the authority of the law, but also the public culture at large had to be based on a foundation other than religion whose contents had become controversial. The new foundation was human nature. Systems of natural law, a natural morality, even a natural religion were designed in order to satisfy that need. Not least of them was the natural theory of government, presented in terms of social contract theories that demonstrated the need for civil government in order to secure individual survival at the price of the natural freedom of individuals, as with Hobbes, or even in order to secure that individual freedom itself within the limits of reason and law, as with John Locke. Wilhelm Dilthey argued successfully that these theories that reconstructed the law, morality, and the foundations of the political order on the basis of the idea of a common human nature, replaced the old religious foundation of society and thus enabled the European nations to put an end to the period of religious wars. The result was the autonomy of secular society and culture with regard to the churches and the religious tradition.

Other theories on the rise of modern secular culture account for its origin as produced by a process of secularization. The most famous of these theories is perhaps Max Weber's work on the origin of modern capitalism. According to Weber, modern capitalism did not develop from purely economic motivations and factors, but its early history depended on the Calvinist doctrine on predestination and its impact on human conduct. Calvin taught that though God's eternal decree on election or repudiation of an individual person remains mysterious, its provision for a particular person can be guessed on the basis of his or her conduct. If they do the works of regeneration, it is likely that such a person belongs to the chosen ones. For the Calvinist believer, then, there exists a strong motivation to produce works of regeneration. According to Protestant ethics, however, these works consist of what one's worldly vocation requires in terms of conscientious observation of professional duties in secular life. Thus Weber assumed that the rational asceticism of the early capitalists had its source in the otherworldly hope of Calvinist spirituality. That spirituality got secularized, however, when its dedication was put in the service of the multiplication of capital, and in that way it produced a system that finally functions independently of the original motivation.

Other applications of the idea of secularization claimed that the modern belief in progress consists of a secularization of the Christian eschatological hope. The hope for progress aims no longer beyond this life, but seeks improvement within this world. Karl Löwith argued that the development of the modern philosophy of history should be regarded as a secularization of the Christian theology of history, the history of salvation. Philosophy of progress replaces the providence of God that had been believed to guide the historical process toward an eschatological consummation, by the predictive power of science and technology bringing about a future of worldly happiness. Science itself was described as having secularized the theological concept of the law by turning it into the idea of eternal laws of nature, and the ideal of an infinite universe in early modern science was considered as the result of a secularization of the earlier belief in the infinity of God.

In all these examples a religious content is transformed into something immanent and this-worldly. Taken together these examples seemed to suggest that modern culture as a whole was the result of a process of secularization, where instead of God, humanity was put in the center and entrusted with the task of directing the course of history, the task which hitherto had been considered the prerogative of God's providence.

The thesis that modernity arose from a process of secularization got criticized by others like Hans Blumenberg, because it puts modern culture under an obligation to its Christian past so as if the substantial contents of modern culture would originally and truly belong not to modernity, but to its Christian predecessor. Against that Blumenberg asserted that modernity emancipated itself from the oppressive claims of the Christian religion, human autonomy forming the core of the modern mind. In effect, this position was not so far removed from that of the theorists of secularization, because their point was also that the religious heritage had been transformed into something else, since humanity rather than God was put in the center.

There is, however, one fateful flaw in the views of both sides, of those who claim that processes of secularization are responsible for the transition from medieval to modern culture but also of those critics who account for that transition in terms of an emancipation from a culture dominated by religion—both these views conceive of the rise of modern culture in terms of a primarily ideological process. In reality, however, the hard facts of war and civil war, the experience of a disruption of social order and peace in consequence of religious controversies produced the occasion that necessitated the transition to a reconstruction of society and public culture that was no longer based on unanimity in religion, since all endeavors to settle the quarrels between religious parties had proven to be in vain. As soon as one recognizes this situation in early modern history, it becomes understandable that at the origin of modern culture people did not mean to turn away from the Christian faith altogether. Emancipation from religion was not the motivation but rather the longterm result of the processes and pressures on enforcing a reconstruction of society on a foundation other than religious faith. Since in the transition to a public culture based on conceptions of human nature rather than religion, a break with Christianity was not intended, it is also understandable that Christian ideas continued to be effective, but were often transformed in the sense of secularized views.

In a Christian assessment of the relationship of modern culture to Christianity, it is particularly important to appreciate correctly the origins of that culture. *First*, the description of the process just offered dissolves the impression, as if modernity from the outset was opposed to the Christian faith. *Second,* the description shows that the visions of Western Christianity in the post-Reformation period and the lack of tolerance in religious controversies were directly responsible for the rise of a secularist culture. That entails the lesson for the Christian churches that unless they overcome those inherited controversies and restore some form of unity among themselves together with a reappropriation of the idea of tolerance to the Christian conception of not only freedom, but of truth itself, they cannot reasonably expect that the exclusion of religious positions from the public square of modern culture be reconsidered. On the other hand, the memory of the role of religion in the origins of modern culture, favors certain conceptions and prejudices about the divisiveness and intolerance of Christian beliefs, entailing also their irrational character and prejudices, that are very difficult to overcome.

## V

A *third* fruit of an appropriate understanding of the way modern culture arose from its Christian past, is an ability to recognize certain ambiguities in basic conceptions of modern culture, ambiguities that are due to a mixture of Christian and non-Christian elements. The most important example of this is the modern idea of freedom. On the one hand, there is a Christian root of the belief that all human persons are born to be free and that therefore their freedom ought to be respected. The Christian meaning of that belief is that all human persons are created in the image of God and meant to enjoy communion with God—in fact it is only communion with God that actually sets us free, according to John 8:36 and Paul, 2 Cor. 3:17. Each human person is created in order to enjoy the freedom that issues from communion with God, but it is only in Christ that such freedom is fully realized through redemption from sin and death. The modern idea of freedom, as it was proposed most effectively by John Locke, differs from the Christian view by focusing only on the natural condition of the human person. It differs also, however, from its other source, the ancient stoic ideas of natural law, since the Stoics considered the original freedom and equality of human beings in the state of nature to be lost because of the necessities of a life in society. It was the Reformation doctrine on the freedom of the Christian that made it possible in Locke's thought to claim the original freedom as an actuality for the present state of human life. And in distinction from later libertarian views of individual freedom, Locke thought that pure freedom is necessarily united with reason and therefore relates affirmatively to law. One can take this position as an echo of the Christian conception that freedom depends on being united with the good and, therefore, with God. The prevailing view of individual freedom in modern societies, however, is the right to do as one pleases. It is not connected with any notion of the good as constitutive of such freedom itself. Any idea of freedom, of course, involves the risk of its abuse, due to the conditions of the incompleteness of human existence in history. The risk of abuse, to be sure, has to be accepted wherever the right to decide independently is granted. But it makes a difference, whether the distinction between use and abuse is observed or neglected in talking about the very constitution of human freedom. If it is observed, freedom cannot be equated with unbridled license. But at this point, the modern use of the idea of freedom is deeply ambiguous, and this ambiguity is characteristic of the ambivalence of secular culture with regard to values in general and to the contents and standards of our cultural tradition in particular. Consequently, a consumer attitude is prevailing far beyond the field of goods that can be obtained or sold on the marketplace. The ambiguous relationship to values and to the cultural tradition is also responsible for the weakness of secularist societies.

## VI

Under the impact of Max Weber the dominate expectation concerning the future of Western culture was, until recently, that secularization would continue to pervade all aspects of society and of individual behavior while religion would be increasingly marginalized. Since two or three decades, however, it has become evident that secularization or, as others put it, progressive modernization of society produces a feeling of meaninglessness in the public arena of society and culture, and such feeling can lead to frustration and irrational, even violent outbreaks against the social system. This is the weakness of secularist culture and the main reason why it is difficult to predict its future. It depends on how long the majority of people will be ready to pay the price of meaninglessness for the space a secularist society offers to the exercise of individual license. As long as this is combined with a situation of comparative affluence, it might be tolerable for a long time. On the other hand, irrational reactions are unpredictable, especially when the feeling of the legitimacy of social institutions erodes. In this precarious situation, the secular societies of the West would do well to pay more attention to the cultural tradition as a source of social stability and especially strengthen the religious roots of their cultural identity.

This is said with regard to the best self-interest of secular society concerning its own stability and longterm survival. Religion as such has little stake in whether such advice is heeded or not. Contrary to anxieties that were widespread a few decades ago among people attached to religious faith, it can be said presently that the future of religion is less precarious than that of the secularist society. Religion is not going to fall victim to progressive secularization. Religion is not going to disappear, because progressive modernization and secularization of society produce a need for sources that can provide meaning for human life, a meaning that we do not give to our life ourselves, but that we have to receive as given by some authority beyond human manipulation. The resurgent interest in religion and in quasi-religious movements that started a few decades ago took secularist intellectuals by surprise, but could have been predicted (and was predicted by some) as an inevitable reaction to secularism.

The renewed interest in religion, however, did not always turn to the Christian churches. In fact, it does so somewhat rarely. Among the reasons of this peculiar fact there seem to be first the widespread prejudices against Christianity as "conventional religion" in the public consciousness of the secularist culture. Therefore, alternative religious options can seem more attractive. A second group of reasons for the fact that the renaissance of religious sensitivity and yearning so often brings water on other mills than the churches may have to do with the ways the churches or many of them respond to the secularist culture. This is the final issue this lecture is turning to: How should the churches relate to the secularist culture?

## VII

The worst way of responding to the challenge of secularism on the part of the Christian churches is to adapt to secular standards in language, thought and the style of life. Unfortunately, many Christians and particularly many clergy consider adaptation to the secular culture a necessary strategy for winning over the people who live in a secularist society and culture. But if members of a secularist society turn to religion at all, they look for something else than they have in that culture. It is the spiritual emptiness of secularism that makes people turn to religion. Therefore, if religion is offered to them in a secularist style, where the religious content is carefully concealed—if it is present at all—it can be counterproductive. This explains, I guess, why in recent decades there has been a decline of membership in mainline churches, while conservative churches grow. What people look for in religion is a plausible alternative or at least a complement to life in a secularist society, and when religion comes to them in a secularist disguise, it is bound to be less attractive.

This argument does not suggest that the churches should stubbornly continue everything that is old-fashioned. The old-fashioned ways of doing things in church may include elements that are really boring or even neurotic. Religion should be presented to members of the secularist society as a vital alternative or complement that is plausible as such. But an alternative to secularism it must be. The presentation of religion, its message and ritual, in secularist disguise inevitably raises the suspicion that the religious substance has sold out and that perhaps the clergy themselves do no longer believe what they are supposed to preach, when they try to get around the hard issues. It is the proclamation of the risen Christ, the joyous manifestation in him of a new life which overcomes death, that the Church owes to the members of a secularist culture.

That the Church in its teaching and lifestyle should withstand the drain of adaptation to the secularist culture, is not an argument in favor of fundamentalism. It is true that fundamentalism in its many forms, with its apparent strength and certitude, is psychologically often successful with persons who suffer from the emptiness and uncertainties of secularism. Where fundamentalism seizes upon a complete population, it can become a terrible power producing a climate of intolerance and violence. But it lacks a deeper plausibility. Therefore, the apparent certitude of fundamentalists is often shallow.

Instead of the fanatic alternative of fundamentalism, the opposition of Christian proclamation and faith to the spirit of secularism should always seek the alliance with reason. That is in keeping with the classical Christian tradition that since the time of the early church used the alliance with reason and with true philosophy to argue for the universal validity of the Christian teaching. In the confrontation with fundamentalism, the secularists are right in exposing irrational fanaticism and intolerance. The Christian opposition to secularism must not lay itself open to charges like that. Rather, Christian teaching may confidently lay claim to the truth that the secularist spirit thinks no longer worth searching for. While at the time of the enlightenment Christian doctrines were challenged in the name of reason and rational truth, contemporary secularism has itself become irrational. It seems the more promising, in such a situation, to renew the old alliance between the Christian faith and reason. Laying claim to reason, however, requires the acceptance of criticism on the side of Christianity itself and an ethos of self-criticism regarding traditional Christian doctrines and forms of spirituality. Even the Bible is not to be exempt from critical inquiry. The acceptance of biblical criticism is an inevitable implication of a renewed alliance between faith and reason. Our Christian confidence in the truth of God and of His revelation should be vigorous enough to suppose that it will not be overcome by any findings of critical inquiry, if only prejudiced forms of criticism are themselves shown for what they are. It would display unbelief, if we felt it necessary to protect the divine truth of the Bible from critical inquiry. Such inquiry can finally only enhance the splendor of the truth of God contained in the biblical writings. Confidence in that truth, however, is what the Christian proclamation and teaching has to live on and to witness to in confronting the challenge of secularism.

# THE SABBATH-REST OF
# THE MAKER OF ALL

STANLEY L. JAKI

Whatever problems a typical reader of Genesis 1 may have with its creation story, they rarely include a puzzlement about God's resting on the seventh day. Yet even on a little reflection that rest reveals the kind of anthropomorphism which all too often aggravates biblical parlance about God. Of course, the image of God taking a rest should seem inoffensive in comparison with the image of God who, according to the second creation story in Genesis 2-3, walks through the Garden of Paradise in the afternoon breeze and replaces with leather garments of His own making the loincloths with which Adam and Eve covered their sense of shame. If there is any human shortcoming involved in God's taking a rest on the seventh day, it is far less shocking than His pretending ignorance of why Adam and Eve felt ashamed on account of their nakedness.

Still, if one is to give, however indirectly, a literal meaning to the assertion about God's taking a rest, it is impossible to avoid the inference that God somehow got tired as He went through His six-day work. The slightest concession to anthropomorphism could then prompt one to picture God in the plainly anthropomorphic posture of toiling and getting tired, distinct as His predicament could be from ordinary human exhaustion.

A most effective antidote to the prompting to think that God is but a superior form of a human being is, of course, on hand in the Decalogue. There the very first commandment, which imposes the duty to worship no gods, only the true God, is bolstered by the prohibition of making graven images of Him: "You shall not carve idols for yourselves in the shape of anything in the sky above or on the

Stanley L. Jaki, a Hungarian-born Benedictine priest, is Distinguished University Professor at Seton Hall University. Winner of the Templeton Prize for 1987, he is an honorary member of the Pontifical Academy of Sciences.

earth below or in the waters beneath the earth" (Exod. 20:4). This prohibition, partly because its transgression entailed death as punishment, forcibly reminded even the most earthy Jew of the non-material nature of the true God. But if God was so different from anything material, what could be the reason for the emphatic assertion that He ceased from His work of six days by taking a rest on the seventh?

The reason has much to do with the justification of the Decalogue's third commandment to turn every seventh day of the week into a holy day: "Remember to keep holy the sabbath day." A justification, and hardly a trivial one, is clearly necessary since the manner of fulfilling the commandment is outlined in severe details: "Six days you may labor and do all your work, but on the seventh day is the sabbath of the Lord, your God. No work may be done then either by you, or your son or daughter, or your male or female slave, or your beast, or by the alien who lives with you" (Exod. 20:8-10). Indeed, the justification given could not have been more exalted in character—the very example set by almighty God is invoked—"In six days the Lord made the heavens and the earth, the sea and all that is in them; but on the seventh day he rested. That is why the Lord has blessed the sabbath day and made it holy" (Exod. 20:11).

Clearly, one is faced here with a divine role model set for man. The point is made even more emphatically when God enjoins Moses to tell the Israelites that the sabbath-rest is both the expression of God's holiness and a means of making the people holy. Moreover, if the same rest is "an everlasting token" between Him and the people, it is only because "in six days the Lord made the heavens and the earth, but on the seventh day he rested at his ease" (Exod. 31:17). Last but not least, the seriousness of the command is conveyed by the threat that anyone desecrating the sabbath would be put to death and "if anyone does work on that day, he must be rooted out from his people" (Exod. 31:14).

A rather different justification of the observance of the sabbath is given in the second version of the Decalogue where only the prohibition to make one's slaves work on the sabbath is mentioned (Deut. 5:15). This difference is, of course, only one of the many that impose the conclusion that the Pentateuch was composed of different parts and over a long period of time. The justification of the sabbath rest with a reference to the example set by God may indeed have been formulated only in post-Exilic times. It could, of course, have circulated orally long before and the prohibition itself could very well be of Mosaic origin. But since that justification is strikingly similar to the concluding phrase of the first creation story, its dating can hardly be separated from the dating of that story.

The dating of the first creation story, as given in Genesis 1 (actually Gen. 1:1–Gen. 2:3), is in part conditioned by the fact that it starkly differs from the story of creation narrated in Genesis 2 and 3. The latter story, because of its primitively narrative character, can readily be assigned to Mosaic times. But the very systematic character of the first creation story betrays the kind of reflection which coincides with later periods in literary development. However, regardless of how the various parts of the Pentateuch are dated, the results would not entail a reconsideration of the main conclusion in this essay.

The usual reason for assigning Genesis 1 to post-Exilic times is its alleged dependence on *Enuma elish*, the Babylonian creation story. Recitals of that story had to be a familiar experience to the Jews in the Exile. But surely, the post-Exilic author of Genesis 1 showed a great originality in eliminating almost everything from that long and convoluted story in order to produce from it, if such was the case at all, his own story in Genesis 1. He kept nothing whatsoever of the long and bloody struggle in which Marduk had to engage before coming to the creation of the world. In that struggle, vaguely symbolic as it could be of the conflict of physical forces or entities, such as sea water, fresh water and mist, Marduk first has to vanquish an armada of gods who rally behind Tiamat the great mother. Moreover, even after his victory Marduk has to use as raw material the chopped up parts of Tiamat's carcass for the formation of the various parts of the world.[1] Clearly, there is something unconvincing in Marduk's producing the sky by his mere breath, a far cry from creation out of nothing.[2]

In Genesis 1 there is no trace of any butchery, any rivalry or any battle. No Leviathan there, no hint of a Chaoskampf[3]—in short, no evidence of any exertion on God's part. God, in Genesis 1, produces everything with an ease which is not disturbed by any competition or difficulty. That consummate ease makes it improper to think that God needed six days for doing His work, let alone for His resting on the seventh. Yet, God emphatically rests on completing His creative work on the seventh day. Here too the difference between Genesis 1 and *Enuma elish* is nothing short of monumental. The Babylonian story is neither structured on a seven-day week, nor does it come to an end with a rest. Rather, on concluding his world-making, Marduk begins a wild celebration with his troupe of victorious gods. Last but not least, in the Babylonian story humans are produced only for the purpose of providing the gods with slaves so that they may continue their carousings at leisure.

This contrast between the endings of these two creation stories should alone discredit efforts to make Genesis 1 appear as a borrowing from Babylonian lore. The idea of such a borrowing is not even bolstered by the fact that in Babylon the king, his magician, and his physician had to abstain from certain acts on the seventh day of each week of two particular lunar months, the Marchesvan and the intercalary month Elul. They must not eat food prepared with fire, must not ride in chariots, must not wear bright garments, and should not exercise authority.[4] But for the ordinary Babylonians life could go on as on any other day of sweat and toil.

Herein lies a major difference with the Jewish sabbath as legislated in the terms set forth above. Also, the Jewish sabbath, unlike the Babylonian, was not fixed to the lunar month. There is no trace in Hamurabi's legislation about the obligation to forgo manual work on the seventh day of the week.[5] The Babylonian *shabattu* and *shapattu* are in all evidence unrelated to the Hebrew *sabbath*. The latter's uniqueness or originality has so far withstood all efforts to present it as a borrowing from other cultures. And the same holds true of Genesis 1 as a whole, although for reasons not necessarily identical with the widely received ones.

One such reason relates to the first phrase of Genesis 1, which contains a detail unnecessarily and unjustifiedly turned into one of its distinctive elements. The detail is the verb *bara*, a verb made mysterious by countless exegetes.[6] They are, of course, right in saying that in all but five of the fifty or so of its occurrences in the Old

Testament, *bara* stands for an action performed by God. But not a few exegetes of that chapter were hardly justified in passing over in silence the fact that there are exceptions to such a use of *bara*. Moreover, the exceptions are not insignificant. Three of them, two in Joshua (Josh. 17:15 and 18), and one in Ezekiel (Ezek. 23:47), are noteworthy partly because they are textually well attested readings. More importantly, the ones in Joshua and the one in Ezekiel are separated by six or seven centuries. In other words, they attest the permanence of the use of *bara* with a purely human connotation—there is nothing divine in the act of cutting down trees on some hilltops, as commanded by Joshua. The same is true of the command of Ezekiel that the bodies of two women of ill repute, representing a faithless Judah and Israel, be cut to pieces.

Tellingly, translators of Genesis 1 are very reluctant to render the first verse of Genesis 1 as, say, "In the beginning God has sundered the heavens [from] the earth."[7] Yet this is what would be required by a strict adherence to the basic meaning of *bara*. Instead, it has become a hallowed custom to render that verse as "In the beginning God *made* the heaven and the earth" which does less injustice to the etymology of *bara* than the phrase, "In the beginning God *created* the heaven and the earth."

After two thousand years of Christian theological reflection, the word creation can emphatically mean only creation out of nothing or *creatio ex nihilo*. This phrase was indeed formulated in early Christian times[8] because it was quickly realized that what Christians meant by creation differed enormously from the "creation" performed by Plato's *demiourgos*, let alone from what was on hand in crassly emanationist, pantheistic cosmogonies. In all these the word *creare* (or its synonyms) could be used, but only insofar as it meant mere growth (*crescere*) from something already there, however embryonically or seminally.

Creation out of nothing is, of course, a supremely effortless act, inasmuch as it totally eliminates all dependence on matter. As such it cannot mean the cutting through of any matter. Of such an absolutely effortless act of creation there is no trace in Genesis 1, free though that chapter is of any crude overtone in reference to a God who works, and performs indeed the greatest conceivable work, the creation of all. But the verb *bara* in the first verse of Genesis 1 still suggests, etymologically at least, that God cut through something, or sundered one part of a thing from another, as He created the all, a totality conveyed by a listing of its two main parts, or the heaven and the earth.

That etymological connotation is much less evoked in the concluding phrase of the creation story. No reference to heaven and earth is made as God is said to have blessed the seventh day and made it holy because on that day God rested "from all his work which God in creating had made (*bara*)." The idea of sundering is only remotely present when the creation of man as male and female is reported in terms of *bara* in verse 27. The immediate context is the making of man in the image of God, where *bara* is used twice.

It would, however, be rash to think that the eminence of man, being made in the image of God, called for the use of *bara* in order to convey an eminently divine action. For *bara* is used in connection with the creation of "the great sea animals and all that creeps, (having) a living soul, which swarmed in the waters according to its kind, and every bird (with) wing according to its kind." By contrast the verb *asa* is used to denote the making of the obviously much more noble items—the sun, the moon, and the stars. By then *asa* had been used in reference to the making of the firmament (verse 7), the most noble part of the Hebrew world edifice. Again, *asa* is used in verse 31, in reference to the totality of what God has made, in jarring dissonance with the use of *bara* in the first verse, where the making of the totality of things is stated. *Asa* is again used when the making of all land animals is mentioned (verse 25). The indiscriminate occurrence of these two verbs in Genesis 1 might by itself discourage efforts to ascribe too readily to *bara* a status with a divine connotation.

No wonder that in translating Genesis 1 into any modern language, scholars have rendered both *bara* and *asa* by the same verb, either to make or to create. The two Hebrew verbs are indeed synonymous to a high degree, whatever their etymological differences. Why then did *bara* earn the special distinction of being used, in the rest of the Old Testament, mostly in connection with an action performed by God? Genesis 1 alone makes it difficult to seek that tie in the relative nobility of the object of God's action. The stars, the moon, and the sun, to say nothing of the firmament, could, even if deprived of any divine status, still seem far nobler than whales and reptiles, yet these lowly creatures and not those heavenly bodies were said to have been made in terms of *bara*.

The answer for the almost invariable connection of *bara* with a divine action may lie in its etymology. Did not the act of slashing carry the connotation of performing something with ease? Analogy with the English idiom, to do something with a flourish, comes to mind. Therefore the first verse in Genesis 1 may mean that "In the beginning God made with the utmost ease the heaven and the earth, that is, the totality of things." However, this point should not be pressed too much. It may be more appropriate to say that *bara* and *asa* were simply used for the sake of stylistic variety.

As was noted above, the expression "heaven and earth" means the totality of things or the universe. It should seem natural that if God is assigned any work, it should not be about some detail but about the whole. The work should have for its object the most encompassing work conceivable, the making of the all or the universe. Indeed, in three steps it is the idea of this totality which is conveyed in Genesis 1. After the general statement concerning the all (verse 1), the work of the second and third days conveys the same totality in terms of the principal parts of the whole or universe as known to the Hebrews. The whole or universe is a tent-like world-edifice, with the floor (the earth) and the roof (the firmament) as its principal parts. Plants come with the earth, because wherever there is moist soil, some vegetation invariably sprouts up.

The same device is used to convey the notion of the all, or universe, in the work of the fourth and fifth days, which witness the production of the main particulars of the principal parts. The stars, sun, and moon are the main particulars of the roof of the cosmic tent, whereas the birds and the fish are the main particulars of the floor region (earth). In fact the author of Genesis 1 gives a hint of his full awareness of using the device in question as he summarizes God's action as follows: "Thus the heaven and the earth and all their array were completed." The word array is a rendering of the

Hebrew *cebaam* (hosts) because of its closeness to *cbi* (ornament, glory) and therefore also translated as decor. Jerome rendered it as *ornatus*, which in turn provided the basis for summarizing the six-day work as *opus divisionis* and *opus ornatus*. Had it been translated, as it certainly could have been, as "particulars," its role in supporting the repeated assertion of totality as the objective of God's work would have sharply stood out.

The stylistic device to convey the idea of the whole by the listing of its main parts is very common in biblical Hebrew. In the Psalms alone[9] one finds a plethora of uses of that device. That all people, or everybody, are meant is conveyed by such expressions "low and high," "rich and poor," "little and great," "the just and the wicked" (Pss. 50, 114, 10). All beasts are meant by "wild and tame" (Ps. 148). All the time, or always, or all seasons, is the meaning of "day and night," "summer and winter," "evening, morning, and noon" (Pss. 1, 74, 55). All movements, all postures are meant by "coming and going," "to walk and to lie down" (Pss. 121 and 139). Psalm 148 is so much structured on this device of stating the whole by listing its main parts as to lend itself to be condensed in a few words: In the heavens/ everybody, everything/ on the earth/ everything/ everybody/ praise the Lord! The similarity with the structure and method of Genesis 1 should seem obvious.

The device, whereby the idea of totality is conveyed in terms of listing the parts, is a staple feature in classical as well as modern languages. Suffice to mention the Greek *en ge kai thalassa*, which is *terra marique* in Latin, and "on land and sea" in English, meaning "everywhere" in each case. In English, this device is on hand in the idiomatic phrases, "lock, stock, and barrel" (the three main parts of a rifle), and "hook, line, and sinker" (three main parts of a fishing gear). Both mean a far greater totality than the entire rifle or the entire fishing equipment.

Curiously, authors, old and new, of books on rhetoric do not pay sufficient attention to this very effective device which may best be called "*totum per partes.*" Whenever they speak of *merismos*, those authors, beginning with Aristotle, have in mind rather the device of *pars pro toto*, which is to convey the idea of totality in terms of one principal part. Exegetes still have to produce a detailed study of the role which the *totum per partes* plays in the Bible as a means of conveying the idea of totality.

The reliance in Genesis 1 on the device *totum per partes* should seem especially significant in view of the surprising rarity of the use of the adjective *khol* (all), a word which, in a context dealing with the all, could be expected to be a dominant feature.[10] Yet *khol* occurs only in reference to the birds and reptiles, and to the plants that nourish man. The only broader use of *khol* occurs only at the end, in reference to the completion by God of all his work and to his resting from all his work.

In Genesis 1 the stating of totality as the object of God's work hinges above all on the use of that stylistic device. It is free from that conceptual obfuscation which is the hallmark of explaining Genesis 1 in terms of myths and legends, both left studiedly undefined. It was not without good reason that Alfred Loisy, a modernist, who would have gladly found in Genesis 1 a legend, called it the most scholastic treatise in the entire Bible.[11] But that almost scholastically logical character of Genesis 1, anchored in the idea of the vastness or total character and of the unrestricted goodness of God's work, remains genuinely biblical, riveted as it is in the biblical notion of the universe. This is why the firmament comes first, as a place closer to the throne of God than the ground, which logically should have come first.

The land animals, which should have come with the fish and the birds as chief particulars of the ground area, come on the sixth day as a background to emphasize the superiority of man and woman over them. Adam conveys his superiority over the animals by naming them. The woman's superiority over the animals is conveyed by the fact that Adam finds no suitable mate for himself among them.

By the sixth day it has been repeatedly stated that whatever God has made is good. The goodness, the perfection of God's productivity, is expressed also in the fact that, as any accomplished architect, God too provides for a manager, for a steward. The perfection of God's work is further conveyed by the fact that, like all sensible architects, He too begins by providing light, before He does anything. By specifying the purpose of the sun to give light, Genesis 1 reveals much of the ambivalence of biblical parlance about light as a special substance, independent of the sun.[12]

Therefore one is entitled, in the context of Genesis 1 alone, to argue that the coming of the light before anything else physical depends above all on the intention of the author of Genesis 1 to present God as a most reasonable worker. As such, God does what every skilled architect or contractor does—He begins by providing light for His work. (He also begins by having on hand the piled up building material—a perspective within which the presence of a primitive chaos [*tohuvabohu*] logically follows.) It makes no sense, that is, biblical sense, to get around the problem of the coming of visible light before the sun by searching in the words "Let there be light!" for a hint of invisible light as assured either in Maxwell's electromagnetic radiation or in the 2.7°K cosmic background radiation. It should now also be very clear why it is abusive to take, however furtively, Genesis 1 for a science textbook in cosmogenesis and biogenesis. It is rather sad that at times well-meaning and devout, first-rate scientists give support to that vagary.[13]

Such an abuse of Genesis 1 did not begin with latter-day creationists. Inasmuch as creationism is an effort to find a concordance between Genesis 1 and the science of the day, practically all the church fathers, all the scholastics, all the reformers and counter-reformers, and all 18th- and 19th-century exegetes of Genesis 1 were guilty on that score.[14] It was not until 1900 or so that the haplessness of this situation began to dawn on leading exegetes.

On the Catholic side, the dawn of awakening was epitomized by F. Hummelauer, professor of Old Testament exegesis at Gregorian University and co-editor of the series *Cursus scripturae sacrae*, to which he contributed the volume on Genesis. There at the end of his survey of the history of interpretations of Genesis 1 he exclaimed: "All is darkness and chaos, whence let light come forth at long last!"[15] Hummelauer felt that there is a solution on hand if Genesis 1 is treated as a series of visions given to Moses. The question whether, among other things, the firmament, to say nothing of the flat earth, was real or merely visionary for Moses, remained unanswered by Hummelauer. Only by doing grave injustice to the very realistic diction of Genesis 1 could one assume that the firmament and the upper waters were not real for the author of Genesis 1, be it Moses or whoever else.

Dissatisfaction with concordist interpretations of Genesis 1 prompted H. Gunkel, on the Protestant side, to give a radically new direction to efforts to cope with that troublesome chapter. He did so, however, by insisting that Genesis 1 be treated as a legend, a myth, to be understood by aesthetic sensitivity.[16] Like many of his Protestant followers (with G. von Rad being most influential among them) and, from the 1940s on, many Catholics as well, Gunkel failed to be specific on the crucial question: What is to be meant by legend and how can it be used in coping with the very realist parlance of the author of Genesis 1 about the external universe? Much less could he explain himself on the subject of aesthetic sensitivity, a very elusive and markedly subjective commodity. The question about the specific nature of a legend or myth was not, for instance, answered in Daniélou's handwaving that the author of Genesis 1 "used its material freely."[17] In fact, the systematic approach of that author, as outlined above, indicates that he did not feel at all free as to what to say and how to proceed. The world as he knew it, and his intent to put across the idea of cosmic totality, set for him a narrowly defined path for presenting his principal message.

That message is the kind of key to Genesis 1 whereby it is unlocked from the fateful grip of comparisons with science, old and new. That principal message is not that God created everything, not that He has full dominance over everything, not even that man was created in His image. Much less is the principal message that man has to be an ecologically minded steward of God's creation, if this message is there at all, and not merely read into it by some new-fangled ecological consciousness.

In Genesis 1, as in any other well-written story, the principal message is disclosed at the very end. At the end of Genesis 1 God is said to have rested on the seventh day, after taking a general look at the completion of a work touching on all things. But this brings back the very first puzzle raised at the very start of this essay: Did God need a rest? Did He spend energy as He worked?

Since both these questions ought to be answered, and for very clear biblical reasons, in the negative, an explanation must be sought in a different direction. This direction readily offers itself as soon as one takes seriously the possibility, a most likely one, that Genesis 1 is a post-Exilic document. The direction is not that very dubious one which is tied to the alleged similarity of Genesis 1 with *Enuma elish*, a story which the Jews could hear *ad nauseam* during their capitivity in Babylon. What really nauseated them was their being under cultural pressure to take the seventh day in the manner in which all others did—by toiling, selling, buying, and carousing.

The immediately post-Exilic times witnessed the birth of modern Judaism, with a central emphasis on the sacredness of the sabbath rest. General neglect of the sabbath observance had already been singled out by Jeremiah as a sufficiently grave offense to bring down "unquenchable fire" on the gates of Jerusalem, whereas its observance could assure that "it remain inhabited forever" (Jer. 17:19-27). In reciting the story of Israel's infidelity, Ezekiel mentions the habitual breaking of the sabbath and lets God recall: "I also gave them my sabbaths to be a sign between me and them, to show that it was I, the Lord, who made them holy" (Ezek. 20:12).

In spite of such prophetic utterances, and in spite of the agonizing lessons of the

Captivity, the observance of the sabbath left much to be desired among the Remnant, whatever the meticulous observance on the part of some. Among the latter were those who, in the Maccabean wars, refused to defend themselves when attacked on the sabbath, a policy which had to be corrected (1 Macc. 2:31-41). No corrective action stemmed the trend which is codified in the section "Shabbath" of the *Mishna*. There among the "forty save one" works prohibited are not only sowing, ploughing, threshing, building, pulling down, and similar patently heavy manual works, but also "making two loops, weaving two threads, separating two threads...writing two letters, erasing in order to write two letters...and taking out aught from one domain into another." Concerning the latter class of work, among the forbidden minute amounts to be moved was the mere drop of oil sufficient to rub the little toe of a one-day old child.[18]

More serious trangressions were the target of Nehemiah's animated pleas on behalf of the holiness of the sabbath which he saw threatened by the mercantile pressures of profit-making. In denouncing them in eight verses (Neh. 13:15-22), practically the grand finale of the historical books in the Hebrew Bible, Nehemiah pronounces eleven times the word sabbath. This makes those eight verses well-nigh unique in the entire Bible with respect to the sabbath and helps one to understand why its observance became so central in the formation of post-Exilic Judaism.

Since in that formation Nehemiah played a central part, it may not seem unjustified to connect the redaction of Genesis 1 with his highly-charged concern for the sacredness of the sabbath. This may also explain the amplification of older texts of Exodus with verses, already quoted, that tie the command about the sabbath observance to God's rest following his act of creation. Such may have been also the context of the addition of various specifics concerning works prohibited on the sabbath. Given at a time when the people lived a nomadic life in the desert, the original Mosaic legislation could hardly contain all the restrictive details on hand in Exodus 20 which is most likely a priestly recension. Most importantly, the obligatory character of those details could be greatly strengthened by a parable in which Almighty God acts as a role model for resting on the seventh day.

Reading Genesis 1 as a parable does not turn it into a legend or a myth. The closer the ties between parables and reality, the more powerful the message. This is why, for instance, the parable of the sower is so effective in its moral message. Genesis 1 would lose much of the effectiveness of its essentially moral message, given in terms of God as a role model for observing the sabbath, if one were to take lightly the realism of its worldview. That view is about the all, as seen by pre-modern man. But, and here comes the biblical saving grace for Genesis 1, that all is merely a reminder that there may be an immensely larger all, not yet known by man, and ultimately known only to God.

In this age, when breakthroughs in scientific cosmology are announced every other month, it is well to recall that scientific cosmologists can never be sure that they deal with the strict totality of things, as they deal with a vast aggregation of galaxies. While an infinite universe was always a sheer extrapolation, never to be viewed from the outside by scientific observers, the finite Einsteinian universe too precludes its scientific verification by external observation. The all, the Universe writ large, remains even in this scientific age the object of an inference, and not a strictly verifiable scientific object.[19]

The same difference exists in the Bible between the *all* known by man at a particular time and the *all* known by God. Awareness of this has telling instances in the Bible. Hanna's exclamation (1 Sam. 2:3) about an all-knowing God witnesses that awareness within the common ranks of the people. On a socially much higher level, there is a similar, though equally spontaneous, instance on hand in Mordecai's prayer where the inference to an all which may surpass the "heaven and earth" lurks between the lines: "You made heaven and earth and every wonderful thing under the heavens. You are Lord of all, and there is no one who can resist you, Lord. You know all things" (Esther 4C:4-5). Against this background, Esther's own exclamation, "you know all things!" may readily appear in its true perspective. Also in post-Exilic times, Susanna takes refuge in the fact that the eternal God knows not only all that is hidden but "all things before they come into being" (Dan. 14:42). These exemplary members of the Jewish people had, in speaking of the all known to God, immensely more in mind than the all that needed to be known about their own particular case. They had in mind that all which it was the privilege of the Almighty to know, an all that could only be approximated, and very remotely at that, by the ever-growing grasp of man's knowledge about things and events.

Had that difference been kept in mind by those learned in biblical lore, much benefit would have been derived both in Jewish and in Christian circles. Among Jews, a barrier would have been set against hairsplitting, so prevalent in Talmudic and Midrashic comments on Genesis 1, concerning physical details of the world-making as described in Genesis 1.[20] The presence of such a barrier would have channelled mental energies for using the sabbath-rest as a spiritual immersion in the meaning of creation. The depths of that immersion were far from being fathomed when Maimonides registered a by then staple view that God commanded resting on the sabbath so that the truth of creation might be pondered and gratefulness for God's kindness be rekindled.[21]

The stifling regulations of *Mishnah* cast their shadows even when a truly deep perspective was voiced. A case in point is the *Horeb* by Samson Raphael Hirsch, chief rabbi in Oldenburg in the 1830s. He viewed the sabbath as a weekly reminder for man about the ever possible misuse of his creative abilities: "What was there to safeguard the world against man? What safeguard that man in his position of honour would not forget God; that he would not look upon the world, which had been entrusted to him to govern according to God's will, as his own property; that in his controlling power over the things around him he would not regard himself as master; and that he would not live in God's world solely according to his human will?" The safeguard was the sabbath-rest. This meant that "even the smallest work done on the Sabbath is a denial of the fact that God is the Creator and Master of the world." However, the work was not physical exertion as such, but any work, however minutely physical which involved a "constructive exercise" of one's intellect: "If you have engendered, without the slightest exertion, even the smallest change in an object for human purposes, then you have profaned the Sabbath, flouted God, and undermined your calling as Jew." And as if to oppose all temptations of modernity, Rabbi Hirsch explicitly specifies man's "technical skill" that assists man's spirit so that he may master the world as the operation to be utterly set aside on the sabbath. By the sabbath-rest man restores the world to God and acknowledges that his own authority over it stands in subjection to Him.[22]

The shift from the last day of the week to the first in the Christian context entailed also a liberation from stifling prohibitions. In line with this, Jerome introduced the distinction between servile and non-servile work as the true meaning of the Mosaic legislation concerning the sabbath-rest. Also, the doctrine of Christ's resurrection included a cosmic perspective on the sabbath-rest, as the pledge of the final restoration of all, a process to which the Christian could rightly contribute, especially with culturally creative work. More recent theological reflections on the resurrection of Christ contain indeed renewed awareness of its ties to the first creation, brought to a close by God's resting on the seventh day.[23]

There are indeed good reasons for believing that a deeper understanding of the sabbath-rest would help to put the six-day creation story in its true perspective—it is a parable with the primary purpose of setting up God as a model in the role of resting after a six-day work. But precisely because the resting is done by God, it symbolizes full spiritual activity. As such it can and should be imitated by man through concentrating on spiritual matters while refraining from all sorts of slaving, toiling and busy-bodying.

Had Genesis 1 been seen in this perspective (which is very different from the perspective of the various steps of His world-making), the lures of concordism might have been resisted from the start, that is, from the late second century that saw the work of the first Christian apologists. The lure was the temptation to have the world-view of Genesis 1 appear to be in conformity with the light which scientific work—first Aristotelian-Ptolemaic, then Copernican, afterwards Newtonian and Laplacian, and in our times Einsteinian and post-Einsteinian—provides about the physical world. For all their awareness of the dangers of that lure, a Basil and an Augustine nevertheless tended to yield to it. The result was a by now two-thousand-year-long bungling with Genesis 1, which brings only discredit to the message about salvation and provides endless grist to the mill of scoffers, often taking cover with copious references to science.

Most importantly, concordist interpretations of Genesis 1 greatly distract from its principal message, which is to see in the Maker of All a role-model for making the sabbath holy. It may be best left for Orthodox Jewish scholars to articulate this connection without imposing prohibitions such as, for instance, the stopping of elevators on the sabbath. As to Christians, their refocusing on that role-model would dampen their enthusiasm for being busy with all sorts of manual projects on weekends. Few factors would indeed counter so effectively the runaway secularization not merely of life but of the lives of Christians as well, than their devout consideration that the Maker of All had set for them the pattern to follow.

Notes

1. Almost invariably ignored by champions of the similarity. A most notable case is provided by the volume *Genesis* (Anchor Bible), translated with an introduction and notes by E.A. Speiser (Garden City, N.Y.: Doubleday, 1962), p. 10.

2. See on this A. Heidel, *The Babylonian Genesis: The Story of Creation*, 2d ed. (Chicago: University of Chicago Press, 1951), p. 21.

3. If Genesis 1 was composed after the Exile, the absence of cosmic struggle in it is all the more noteworthy. Not only did the author of Genesis 1 give wide berth to what had already been available in Isaiah chapter 27, but also to two post-Exilic Psalms, 74(75) and 89(90), in both of which God's crushing of the heads of Leviathan (Rahab) is given with succinct vividness as an expression of God's superiority over whatever dark forces there may be operating in nature.

4. See R. North, "The Derivation of Sabbath," *Biblica* 36 (1955): 182-201.

5. Those who overemphasize the dependence of the Mosaic legislation on Hamurabi's laws, in order to undermine the possibility of revelation, are, as a rule, strangely silent on the total absence in that famed Babylonian text to any reference to a rest on the last day of the week. It hardly testifies to much thinking that this applies to the most widely read English version of Hamurabi's laws, *The World's Earliest Laws* by C. Edwards (London: Watts & Co, 1934), which is number 43 in *The Thinker's Library*.

6. Such as W. Eichrodt and P. Heinisch. Their efforts partly hinge on the rather unconvincing implicit assertion that the meaning of a Hebrew verb can noticeably change when used in some (Kal and Nifil) and not in other tenses.

7. Even such a resolute champion as P. Beauchamp of the idea that biblical creation is a separation is reluctant to obey the full logic of his position in this respect. See his *Création et séparation: Etude exégétique du chapitre premier de la Genèse* (Paris: Aubier Montaigne, 1969).

8. This was done with a particular force by Tertullian.

9. For other examples, see my *Genesis 1 through the Ages* (London: Thomas More Press; New York: Wethersfield Institute, 1992), pp. 281-86.

10. As noted by H. Ringgren in his article *khol* in *Theologisches Wörterbuch zum Alten Testament* (Stuttgart: W. Kohlhammer, 1982- ), vol. 4, col. 148.

11. A. Loisy, *Les mythes babyloniens et les premiers chapitres de Génèse* (1901; repr. Frankfurt: H. Saamer, 1916), p. 25.

12. That independence was emphasized, more on the basis of Egyptian than of biblical documents, by W.F. Albright, in section 1, on chaos and the origin of light in Genesis, of his essay, "Contributions to Biblical Chronology and Archeology," *Journal of Biblical Literature* 43 (1924): 363-69.

13. The widest circulation was given to that misunderstanding by the famous astronomer, Sir James Jeans, in his *The Mysterious Universe*, first published in 1929. There the reference to the transformation of matter into radiation is followed by a prominent scientist's most unscientific exegesis: "These concepts reduce the whole universe to a world of light, potential or existent, so that the whole story of its creation can be told with perfect accuracy and completeness in the six words: 'God said, Let there be light' " (p. 3). In recent years, A. Penzias, a devout Orthodox Jew and a Nobel laureate, made a similar connection in the pages of the *New York Times* (March 12, 1978, p. 1).

14. As argued throughout my *Genesis 1 through the Ages*.

15. F. Hummelauer, *Commentarius in Genesim* (Paris: P. Lethielleux, 1895), p. 68.

16. H. Gunkel, *The Legends of Genesis*, tr. W.H. Carruth (Chicago: Open Court, 1907).

17. J. Daniélou, *In the Beginning...Genesis I-III*, with a foreword by G. Sloyan (Baltimore: Helicon, 1965), p. 29.

18. *The Mishna*, translated from the Hebrew with introduction and brief explanatory notes by H. Danby (London: Oxford University Press, 1933), p. 106. Similar details fill for the most part

the entire section "Shabbath" pp. 100-120.

19.  See my *Is there a Universe?* (Liverpool: Liverpool University Press; New York: Wethersfield Institute, 1993), the enlarged text of the Forwood Lectures for 1992 delivered at that University.

20.  For details, see my *Genesis 1 through the Ages*, pp. 43-45.

21.  *The Guide for the Perplexed*, tr. M. Friedländer (1881; 2d rev. ed.; New York: Dover, 1956), p. 219 (part II, ch. 31).

22.  S.R. Hirsch, *Horeb: A Philosophy of Jewish Laws and Observances*, tr. I. Grunfeld (London: Soncino Press, 1962), 1:62-64. The work first appeared in German in 1837 as an effort to specify the duties of Jews living in the Diaspora.

23.  Thus par. 106, dealing with the observance of Sunday, in "The Constitution on the Sacred Liturgy" of Vatican II.

# ON THE LEGALITY AND MORALITY OF PHYSICIAN-ASSISTED SUICIDE

DAVID J. BAGGETT

*There is but one truly serious philosophical problem, and that is suicide. Judging whether life is or is not worth living amounts to answering the fundamental question of philosophy.* — *Albert Camus*

In the state of Michigan, a battle is raging over the activity of Dr. Jack Kevorkian. A former pathologist, he began medically assisting suicides in 1990 to enable suffering, terminally ill patients to end their lives. In March 1993, the Michigan state legislature banned assisted suicides, a law specifically aimed at Kevorkian. What is happening in Michigan, largely inspired by the furor surrounding "Dr. Death," is a microcosm of things to come in the United States. The scenario in Michigan concerning physician-assisted suicide (PAS) or medicide is not new, but has been fanning the flames of the debate elsewhere over this practice, a debate that will undoubtedly in time take on national and international proportions. The Hemlock Society, which promotes the legalization of PAS for the terminally ill, has upwards of 50,000 members, and recently two states voted down "right to die" initiatives by only narrow margins.[1]

More and more people are coming to believe that it is their right to end their lives when they wish by this intentional means. If assistance from a doctor is required, the doctor should not be punished. PAS, so the argument goes, should not be legally banned. Those who oppose the legalization of PAS and thereby support the banning of it, on the other hand, claim that the state would make a

*David J. Baggett teaches philosophy at the University of Michigan–Dearborn in Dearborn, Michigan. He is also a Ph.D. student at Wayne State University in Detroit.*

mistake if it does not take a stand against it, and inaction would establish a dangerous precedent by essentially sanctioning the deliberate taking of life.

PAS obviously transcends the scope of Kevorkian and his lawyer, Geoffrey Fieger. A more thorough treatment would engage the more thoughtful Dr. Timothy Quill, author of *Death and Dignity: Making Choices and Taking Charge*. However, since Kevorkian and Fieger represent such central figures in this emerging debate, it is instructive to take them as somewhat paradigmatic of this movement. Kevorkian sees himself as the leading proponent of an important historical revolution, in which the taboo surrounding death will finally be removed.

He has apparently received numerous requests for assistance. He screens out many of them, ostensibly considering only those which meet the following criteria: the patient must be suffering from a fatal or irremediable condition from which he or she will never recover, the patient's family must entirely agree, the patient's medical condition must be verifiable by Kevorkian, a psychological consultation when appropriate and the patient must never waver.

In an effort to explore a few of the relevant issues involved in this admittedly morally ambiguous question, let us critically examine a representative argument in favor of PAS, which typically goes something like this: People have the right to end their own lives, and to enlist medical professionals to help, when pain becomes too great to bear and life's quality is thereby reduced to an unconscionable level. Those, myself included, who would deny this right are, according to Fieger, religiously motivated fanatics who simply wish to impose their provincial views on others. Three important issues raised by this stance of PAS supporters are the following: What should be thought of those religiously motivated opponents of PAS? Is it truly people's right to end their lives when they wish with a doctor's assistance? And is the rationale of reducing pain sufficient basis on which to risk legalization of PAS?

RELIGIOUS BIAS

What should be thought of religiously motivated opponents of PAS? A large number of the most vocal opponents of PAS are, at some level, religiously motivated. Among supporters of PAS there has been a concerted effort to capitalize on the religious nature of this resistance. Among the likes of Fieger is a conscious and deliberate attempt to portray the opponents of PAS as zealous religionists far to the political right of mainstream America. These fanatical reactionaries, the argument goes, though unwilling themselves to change, are exceedingly willing to impose their narrow views on others. At the most elementary and obvious level, this effort is an example of the logical fallacy *argumentum ad hominem*, which assumes that discrediting a person thereby discredits his or her arguments.

A more legitimate critique of religious motives questions their value in a pluralistic society. In age when the wall of separation between church and state is assiduously maintained, and when the need for tolerance and openness to a broad spectrum of ideas is emphasized, religion has taken on a pejorative tone in public discourse. The trend is toward increasingly permissive legislation, including the legalization of PAS, and personal choice seems to be the dictated conclusion of any social issue involving religious conviction. All it takes for an issue to be decided on the basis of personal choice is the characterization of the debate as religious in character, at which point it is automatically assumed that nothing more needs to be said. If classical theism or traditional religion is involved, then the question is answered: personal choice has priority.[2]

Certainly this debate entails more than religious considerations alone. Relevant to this debate, for instance, are agreed upon nonreligious standards to test consequences. But this debate remains in need of being informed by religion. An issue like PAS or euthanasia requires societies to decide on a collective moral vision. Christians in this society have always been passionate players in that process, and those of every creed must continue to be involved and included. Unfortunately, this culture is quickly forfeiting its intellectual capacity to acknowledge the relevance of transcendent and religiously based normative moral codes to public discourse. Richard John Neuhaus, one of today's foremost authorities on religion in contemporary society, stresses that laws, to retain legitimacy, must be seen to be coherently connected with basic presuppositions about right and wrong, good and evil.[3] He warns that morality becomes mere sentimentality when its religious foundations and theological underpinnings are lost, but recently we have too often uncritically assumed that religiously based moral concerns can no longer be binding on our public ethic.[4] While that has taken place, the resultant moral void has simply been dogmatically filled in with other moral postulates as greedy for transcendence as anything religion can muster. The public square detests a moral vacuum.

Society's uncritical relegation of religion to a place of irrelevance is having numerous harmful consequences, and those who argue that religious conviction ought to be a disqualification from the public debate are laboring under fundamental misunderstandings. This bias against religion will not only sustain the dichotomy between the institutions of church and state, but will drive a wedge between the laws of the land and religiously rooted moral values. Whenever this happens, potentially positive legislation and constructive influence can be lost simply because they are construed as too suggestive of religion. Imagine the result if Dietrich Bonhoeffer's opposition to Hitler, Martin Luther King's battle for equal rights or William Wilberforce's fight against slavery had been silenced and consigned to irrelevance just because they were in part spurred by religious conviction.

If the attempt to portray PAS as a *legal* debate with no room for religion is one attempt to silence religious resistance to PAS, another attempt is to portray the debate as a *scientific* and *medical* matter. Dr. Kevorkian has said that he will "do what a doctor should do: alleviate the suffering of the human being in front of me if it's justified medically." Notice that the alleged basis for his actions is *medical*, not *moral*. His lawyer has similarly asserted that it is inappropriate to "inject a matter of faith with a purely medical and scientific issue." The clear implication is that this debate is a medical and scientific debate alone with no room for religion, faith claims or traditional morality.

This is confused thinking. By its nature, science alone is not equipped to handle moral, philosophical or metaphysical inquiry. The debate over PAS involves these very questions. The insistence that science alone answer the moral questions about

PAS assumes a mistaken view of what science does. Science deals with the empirically verifiable and quantifiably measurable, not normative and prescriptive questions of ethics. Whether anything exists outside science's necessarily truncated vision is not a question it can answer, nor one it should be expected to answer. The evidence that science offers concerning our ultimate questions, such as detectable patterns of regularity or the auspicious conditions for human life, is necessarily ambiguous and inconclusive.

Arguing that theological considerations be bracketed out of this debate is simply naive at best, patently dishonest at worst. Doctors should not be the only ones doing medical ethics. Their insights and facts are crucial, but without religious convictions, logical distinctions and ethical discussions, the prior philosophical and theological assumptions of doctors may be advanced dogmatically in the name of science and uncritically accepted. That includes Dr. Kevorkian, who hastens to give primacy to his own "scientific" moral ideals and expects the laws to live up to those standards, while those with a "religious" moral vision are supposed to keep quiet and, preferably, out of the public debate.

Likewise, Howard Simon, executive director of the American Civil Liberties Union, concurs with Kevorkian when he claims that opposition to legalizing PAS on theological grounds is illegitimate. Certainly, however, Simon must be aware of his own guiding truth claims and ideological biases, such as when he claims, echoing Kevorkian's sentiments, that "the right to control our own lives...belongs to each of us" and "it is my life and the decision should be mine." These are ambitious theological assertions in their own right, as are any fundamental presuppositions which incline us toward one side of this debate or the other. Simply because his propositions reflect a "secularistic theology," as it were, does not exempt them from scrutiny. And just because the assumptions of some are fueled by religious conviction and tempered by traditional morality does not mean they ought to be decried.

As a society we are fast losing our language for moral discourse. And by ruling out of court as irrelevant any religious morality, a great historical source of our public ethos in this country, we are now more and more refusing to contend with the complexities of ethical conundrums. The probable basis on which an issue like PAS will eventually be decided will be very narrow, and it will likely be this: PAS safeguards our rights, while a law against it would reduce our freedoms. Is that the extent of collective moral imagination and discussion of which this culture is capable?

RIGHT TO DIE

In the fall of 1993, my father suffered and died from an acute case of lymphoblastic leukemia. In his final weeks, his condition deteriorated daily. The final two weeks rendered him unconscious much of the time, delirious and disoriented from the cumulative effect of chemotherapy, internal hemorrhaging, the cancer itself and the several medications being administered. When his time of death arrived, the family had already done much of their mourning. Seeing him dying like that seemed worse than the actual death itself.

My father's suffering could have been worse. It certainly could have been better, but it could have been substantially worse in terms of intensity and duration. As my father suffered and my family suffered along with him, I thought about physician-assisted suicide at times. I was not giving it serious consideration in this case, but was attempting to understand its appeal in the lives of those who have had to endure prolonged periods of suffering. It is not difficult to see why a relatively painless and immediate death can seem so much better than continuing in horrendous pain (though modern palliatives make such cases rare).

But I hesitate affirming a legislative sanction of physician-assisted suicide. Among my reservations is a serious concern over the way rights language has been employed in this debate, sometimes clouding the issues considerably and avoiding important questions altogether. In this section I would like to discuss this rights language in moral discourse generally and in the PAS debate particularly, pointing out a few of the limitations, assumptions, and implications of its common usage.

Supporters of PAS submit that it protects the "right to die" of human beings. The point they are stressing is people's right to die when they *choose* to die. Expressed less euphemistically, those like Kevorkian and Fieger are asserting people's right to kill themselves and to enlist others' help when required. It is not simply the negative right of refusing life-preserving treatment, but the positive, legislatively sanctioned right of officially assisted suicide. That people have the right to commit suicide, even with the help of a licensed health care professional, is becoming an accepted moral postulate, increasingly treated as a self-evident proposition, within the conventional wisdom and reigning "plausibility structures" of this culture. It is usually stated dogmatically, thereby begging a most important question of this debate: Is suicide our right, and does it include the right to enlist the assistance of others?

The assumption that moral debates can be reduced to the level of rights is widespread, a trend concerning which I hold some reservations. I should therefore quickly preface this discussion by stressing that I am not yet convinced of the validity and soundness of the arguments in favor of conducting moral dialogue exclusively (or even primarily) in rights language. Such discourse typically assumes that the world is constituted under adversarial power structures and attempts to construct an individualistic approach to ethics, while yielding conclusions far-reaching and communal in scope. Rights do not exist in a vacuum, not even private rights, for to assert a right is also to impose an obligation on our society to provide means for the exercise of that right. Rather than reinforcing individualism when a private right is societally affirmed, that society incurs upon itself at the moment of legislation the obligation to provide the suitable means for its citizens to enjoy that right.

That the question of rights has generally come to be seen as the legitimate focus of the PAS debate is undeniable, however. Interestingly, both sides of the debate often employ rights language. The Hemlock Society, which promotes the legalization of PAS for the terminally ill, speaks of a "right to die," while their strongest opponents are typically self-avowed "right to life" proponents. The present ban against PAS in my home state of Michigan was temporarily repealed when Judge Cynthia Stephens decided that "the right of self-determination includes the right to choose to cease living." By some estimates, about eighty percent of the population of the state of

Michigan believe that human beings possess a "right to die" and that legislation sanctioning PAS ought to be adopted. This figure is usually reflected among my philosophy students at the university where I teach, with about four out of five initially affirming PAS because "that's our right."

An important reason why one's right to die is often uncritically accepted today is this society's cultural climate. It is a culture averse to imposition. Since anything that smacks of imposition is anathema, the banning of PAS has an inherent strike against it from the outset. By its nature, it is a nonpermissive law and is thus characterized by its opponents as an imposition of religious values and an infringement of rights. Within our contemporary moral context, where primacy is often given to individual and private rights, it is small wonder that PAS is finding an increasingly receptive audience. Considered carefully, this cultural climate offers little reason to assume that suicide is indeed our right. It certainly helps explain why rhetoric appealing to rights language in the PAS debate is effective persuasion for so many, but the prior question of whether suicide is indeed a right has still not been answered.

The swelling popular conviction that suicide is a right has usually resulted less from good reasons and logical arguments than from a brute assumption being absorbed into the working mentality of our culture. When pressed, one reason that may be offered for such a right is that suicide as an option is an implication of human freedom. We possess a free will with which we can justifiably make our own decisions about our lives, it is argued. This rationale, though, is clearly inadequate, confusing free will with other types of freedom, and assuming that what we can freely choose of our own volition should necessarily be politically, ethically, and legally permissible. Quite obviously that is not the case. Something which we possess the capability of doing is not thereby a right. Libertarian freedom, if it exists in the face of the challenge of determinism, implies neither political freedom nor moral license necessarily.

It may be suggested that a right to die can be gleaned from the *Karen Ann Quinlan* case and subsequent rulings which have established the right under certain circumstances to be disconnected from artificial life support systems. This procedure has come to be known as passive euthanasia, allowing death to take place naturally. Justice Scalia, in the *Nancy Beth Cruzan* decision, equated the termination of life support with ordinary suicide, collapsing any distinction between passive euthanasia and PAS. However, it does good to recall that Scalia was the only justice to do so. The assertion that denial of life-saving medical treatment by a competent patient constitutes suicide has been largely rejected logically and legally, and for good reason. Suicide involves active steps taken to induce death, while passive euthanasia affirms the causality of the underlying disease as the agency of a person's death. The Michigan ban on PAS that has been alternately legislated and struck down specifically distinguishes PAS from "withholding or withdrawing medical treatment."

Some opponents of PAS strongly support passive euthanasia for similar reasons they oppose PAS. As my father's condition worsened, the family had to make a decision regarding his "code status." As an opponent of PAS, I was also a strong voice in support of declaring my father's status "no code." That meant, in case of cardiac arrest, for instance, he would not be resuscitated. Doctors and nurses would have made pain management and comfort care their priority, *not* the prolonging of his life at any cost. With everything else my father had experienced in recent years medically, and now with him suffering from a fatal disease, I and my family decided that it was time to draw the line in terms of how much we could reasonably expect medicine to do. PAS supporters neglect doing this, it seems, believing that a doctor's obligation is not only to prolong life and minimize pain, but to help in the taking of life when all else fails. The lesson to learn from vexing moral dilemmas introduced by too great a faith in medicine is to draw the line earlier, placing *less* trust in medicine, not to expect medicine to solve the problem that it has helped create (usually at the insistence of patients' families).

Some suggest that a right to die is presupposed in ongoing medical techniques. Such a challenge attempts to blunt distinctions between PAS and what is already accepted medical practice. In attempting to alleviate pain, doctors often administer substantial doses of analgesics and, in doing so, sometimes hasten death. One of the points of resistance to laws against PAS in the medical profession is concern that such laws may impede current medical procedures. However, a traditionally honored distinction can be upheld by means of the doctrine of *double effect*, traceable to Aquinas. This distinction points out the difference between primary and secondary effects, arguing that culpability not be extended to secondary effects unintended by our actions. Substantial doses of palliative therapies requested by patients may occasionally hasten death, but death in such cases is an inadvertent effect of the primary goal of pain relief. PAS *intentionally* induces death rather than secondarily and inadvertently effecting it, distinguishing PAS from ambitious palliative therapy.[5]

Suppose this suggestion: suicide is at least our *legal* right since so many states have struck down legislation making it illegal. In response, I would ask this question: Does the absence of legislation against suicide make it our right? Perhaps another important reason for not making suicide illegal other than the desire to provide its sanction is that criminal punishment is virtually ineffectual as a deterrent to suicide. In this case, another reason is obvious: there is no way to punish a successful victim of suicide! The fact that a law against suicide cannot be enforced does little to confirm suicide as our right, particularly given this culture's formal efforts to avoid suicide. If suicide has been given our blessing, why have state legislatures found it in the public interest to dissuade such behavior by funding ambitious suicide prevention programs and forbidding assisting in a suicide?

To call our presumed right to die into question almost seems a waste of time, but it happens to be that little piece of question-begging with which many opponents of PAS have to differ. This alleged right usually functions as the crucial unquestioned premise in the argument for PAS, without which the argument fails. To say "I have a right to end my life when I wish" is easy, while testing the legitimacy of such a claim becomes more involved. We are driven to foundational questions about communal responsibilities, limitations on personal rights, the significance of death and the appropriateness of suicide.

What exactly is meant by saying that we have this moral right to choose when to die? A right is something one is entitled to, that to which one has a just and proper

claim, and implies a principle of congruity and appropriateness. It is something appo-
site to us. The rights a society argues for thereby reveal its anthropology; the basic
human, moral, legal rights a society *believes* it possesses reflect what it *thinks* of
humanity. The rights people *actually* possess are dictated by the *true nature* of humanity, which may or may not be accurately reflected in what a society believes. The discussion of anthropology concerning human nature is prior to the decision about
human rights, and has to take place at the level of worldview.

Representatives from a broad array of worldviews are encouraged to enter the public debate over PAS and voice their convictions and concerns. They are at liberty to
convince the populace of the wisdom or compassion of PAS, or lack thereof, by the
power of their ideas and cogency of their arguments. This courtesy should be extended to the spectrum of worldviews, from theists and atheists to existentialists, Kantians
and humanists. The debate over PAS features an appeal to our ultimate commitments,
our most basic ethical convictions and most deeply cherished values. Satisfactorily
answering whether or not we as a culture wish to affirm that suicide is a basic and
fundamental right requires the participation of everyone, the formation of a consensus and the clearest and best of arguments all around.

The dogma that people have the right to end their lives when they so choose presupposes a humanistic understanding, according to which human beings are the masters of
their own destiny, entirely autonomous and independent. This approach should not be
exempt in the public arena from the same critical scrutiny rightly aimed at all other possible worldviews. In contrast to humanists, theists often question those Homo sapien-
centered assumptions, positing instead that humankind is God's *creation,* and as created
beings, essentially dependent on God, they are subject to God's sovereignty. According to
most theistic conceptions of humanity, no such right to commit suicide exists. Such a
right would usurp God's authority, exceed the prerogatives of human freedom and violate the prohibition against murder that the Judeo-Christian ethic, for instance, teaches—
an ethic that has long served to inform public discourse in this culture.

This culture *can* discard such theistic perspectives as archaic and outdated if it will;
the question is whether it *should.* To assume that all traditional moral convictions are
necessarily inferior to the "liberated" ethics of today is potentially the apex of arro-
gance, an instance of what has been called "chronological snobbery."

Unlike life, liberty and the pursuit of happiness in the Declaration of Independence,
suicide is usually not touted as an unalienable right with which we have been endowed
by our Creator. Kevorkian certainly would not attribute such a right to God; his worldview is succinctly put in his answer to the question of what happens to us after we die:
"You rot." Assuming human rights are either intrinsic or conferred, then, that would
leave the so-called right to die as a necessary part of humanity or personhood. Those
who are inclined to deny such a right, on the other hand, see PAS as contrary to human
nature. Theists generally assume that the wisdom of God's moral laws is evident in the
way they accord with both nature in general and human nature in particular.

Those truly individualistic impulses and instincts not to be denied within us usually do not have to do with our rights so much as with our natural desire as human
beings to survive. J. Gay-Williams, reflecting on euthanasia, has argued that

Every human being has a natural inclination to continue living. Our reflexes and responses fit us to fight attackers, flee wild animals, and dodge out of the way of trucks. In our daily lives we exercise the caution and care necessary to protect ourselves. Our bodies are similarly structured for survival right down to the molecular level. When we are cut, our capillaries seal shut, our blood clots, and fibrogen is produced to start the process of healing the wound. When we are invaded by bacteria, antibodies are produced to fight against the alien organisms, and their remains are swept out of the body by special cells designed for clean up work.

It is enough, I believe, to recognize that the organization of the human body and our patterns of behavioral responses make the continuation of life a natural goal. By reason alone, then, we can recognize that euthanasia sets us against our own nature.... Euthanasia involves acting as if this dual nature—inclination towards survival and awareness of this as an end—did not exist. Thus, euthanasia denies our basic human character and requires that we regard ourselves or others as something less than fully human. Euthanasia does violence to this natural goal of survival.[6]

This innate desire we have to preserve and sustain life has long been encapsulated in the Hippocratic Oath doctors take. Euthanasia and PAS violate the natural inclination people have to preserve life and safeguard society. Deep within us are a desire and sense of responsibility to heed our will to live and thereby cultivate the fabric of society rather than to militate against and undercut that through an individualistic warrant for suicide. How do proponents of PAS justify their exclusively individualistic orientation when faced with the inherent sense of social responsibility that we all feel and that most all cultures have cherished?

It suffices to say that the right to die, a crucial premise in the case for PAS, does not deserve its status as an unapproachable, unassailable verity. In fact it is but one dubious tenet among others in a worldview that claims an exalted view of humankind, but which actually leaves an ever decreasing set of safeguards in place for the innocent and most helpless of the species. Opponents of PAS seriously question whether the arena of death is one in which finite human beings exercise legitimate and exclusive autonomy. The words of Gloucester from *King Lear* still ring clear: "We must endure our going hence even as our coming hither."

## SLIPPERY SLOPE

If this society decides to legalize PAS, it will institutionalize a certain rejection of the prohibition against murder by sanctioning assistance in self-murder. Such a decision will largely be based on an *act-utilitarian* ethic contending that the elements that make an act right or wrong are not the intrinsic features of the act, but the consequences of the act. Assisted self-murder will be legalized in certain cases because in those cases the ends will have been deemed to justify the means. Rather than a rule-based orientation, utilitarianism will have become the dominant ethical approach of the legislators, at least in the case of PAS. The opinion of many people is that it is high time for this transition to take place, and for utilitarianism to be accorded its special place of honor in the formation of our public ethic.

Act-utilitarianism remains a problematic method of formulating a public ethic, however, because an exclusive regard for each action's consequences, over against general *prima facie* rights and wrongs, makes today's legislative decisions a major, not to mention laborious, guessing game. Decisions which are made to minimize suffering, given the limited knowledge and perspective we have, may turn out tomorrow to have been entirely mistaken, a notorious epistemological difficulty of utilitarianism. What goes especially unquestioned is whether the utilitarian denial of ethical norms is a prudent way in which to achieve the best of consequences.

Often overlooked is the fact that adherents of traditional rule-based ethics are usually at least as concerned with the consequences of actions as utilitarians are, sometimes more so. Although traditionalists believe in the existence of objective moral standards, they also happen to be convinced that it is the faithful following of those ethical norms, in general, by which the overall best consequences are finally secured for all concerned.[7] According to this understanding, the deleterious consequences of an immoral action are not merely an incidental effect but a manifestation of the action's ethically deficient nature, a function or an internal component of evil, if you will. An intimate relationship thus operates between an action's intrinsic moral features and its ultimate consequences, so that certain behavior is not wrong simply because it results in hurt, but rather it often results in harm because it is actually bad. A society which institutionalizes the rejection of an inherently right moral precept or principle, or embraces a wrong one, places itself at a grave risk to reap the destructive whirlwind of consequences which will invariably flow out of that decision.[8]

This analysis can be applied to PAS in a most socially relevant fashion. On *rule-utilitarian* grounds alone, if it could be effectively argued that the legalization of PAS could and most probably would have devastating results, that alone should be a sufficient reason to ban it. Alleged rights, such as suicide, have been denied to exist in the past when they were perceived to be inherently wrong and such restrictive legislation was deemed to serve the public interest. Certain rights are also denied to exist when their probable result would be the fundamental undermining of a culture. Government has the responsibility to impose legitimate limitations on personal freedoms when necessary to safeguard the welfare of a society.

Many attempts have been made to delineate the potential harmful effects of euthanasia and PAS. These are arguments which appeal to what is called a "slippery slope." The idea behind such arguments is that once we have started down an incline, by legalizing PAS for instance, there is no putting a stop to the momentum of the resultant downward motion. Some would call such reasoning fallacious, as some appeals to slippery slope arguments against PAS undoubtedly are, some being mere "scare tactics." However, not all of them are, and the fact is that legitimate concerns exist over the kind of precedent the legalization of PAS would set.

It is far from my intention to provide an exhaustive catalogue of all the possible negative consequences of legalizing PAS. A few that others have elaborated on include the possible decline in overall medical care, the corruption of medical practice, damage to patients' confidence in physicians, the prospect of PAS becoming the only feasible medical "treatment" for the poor, the making of killing increasingly acceptable and routine and the extension of PAS to include the chronically depressed or those who simply feel useless or like a burden (note the dehumanizing connotations in such labels as "useless" or "burden").

Such speculations and conjectures about worst-case scenarios after the legalization of PAS are often dismissed categorically by avid PAS supporters. However, it is they themselves who have chosen consequentialism as the most reliable route for finding the right public policy. If they are true to their principles, they should be as concerned with the potentially damaging results of legalizing PAS as anyone. Their natural rejoinder is that they endorse legalization only under clear restrictions and guidelines which would regulate the practice and minimize harmful effects or abuses.

The logic of PAS itself defies such regulation, however. For if suicide is a right intrinsic to human nature, with what substantive justification can we discourage suicide for any reason whatsoever? When human autonomy justifies PAS, as a growing portion of this society believes, then any competent person is accorded the "privilege." The lesson will be conveyed through the legalization of PAS that suicide is the proper, or at least a legitimate, response to a life subjectively and individually deemed below an acceptable quality level. Suicide could well become the epidemic result of this implicit societal teaching, and it would not be long before the integrity of the whole culture could be seriously violated. Teenagers, among whom suicide is already rampant, would essentially be issued a societal sanction to opt for suicide rather than enduring their temporal troubles. The suicide rate today among the elderly has already surpassed that of teenagers, a tragedy that would be only exacerbated by PAS.

Another portion of this culture's population considers mercy, not autonomy, to be the salient rationale for PAS, the more utilitarian oriented basis. But once we have formally substituted the importance of the quality of life as we judge it for the importance and dignity of life itself, how can we impose a limit on the logical implications and practical ramifications of such a decision? On what nonarbitrary grounds can we continue to uphold even those screening criteria of Kevorkian's? How can we withhold death from those most in need of it just because they are no longer competent to assert their wishes? Once we lift up the immediate reduction of pain or, even better, its total elimination as the supreme virtue and sublimest goal of our public ethos, does PAS become not only the privilege but the mandate? Do we not confer upon ourselves an ever-increasing responsibility to resolve pain by bringing about death? Pain is not only part of dying, it is part of living.

If PAS by nature is beyond regulation, *now* is the time for us to realize that. After medicide is characterized as a right, no reversal of course is realistic, no matter how painful the path we traverse. Any attempt to do so would simply produce an outcry of protest, just the way prohibition did or a repeal of abortion rights would today. Once legislatively affirmed and societally appropriated, rights become entrenched in our mindset and practically impossible to remove.

Precedent, the crucible of experience, shows the ease with which PAS leads to voluntary active euthanasia and, eventually, to involuntary active euthanasia, including the physically disabled, the mentally incompetent and those too expensive to treat. In Holland, where PAS has been officially tolerated, three percent of all deaths are now directly caused by doctors. That percentage would translate into over 60,000 deaths caused annually by doctors in this country.[9] What is more, Dutch physicians are now performing more than two times more involuntary euthanasia than voluntary, an unpalatable statistic for the empirically minded utilitarian to swallow.[10] A 1991 study found that in one year more than 1,000 Dutch patients incapable of giving consent died at the hands of their doctors, demonstrating that PAS resides at the threshold of euthanasia, another terrifying slippery slope.[11]

Former Surgeon General C. Everett Koop writes

> I am convinced that in the 1930s the German medical sentiment favoring euthanasia (even before Hitler came to power) made it easier for the Nazi government to move society along that slippery slope that led to the Holocaust. The German euthanasia movement started with defective babies, then reached out to eliminate the insane, then to those suffering from senile dementia, then to patients with advanced tuberculoses, to amputees deemed of no further service to the Reich, to Gypsies, to Poles, and finally to Jews. The Holocaust was upon us.[12]

PAS essentially involves a contract between a patient and his doctor for a service to be rendered that will culminate in one party in the contract dying. Even though this may be a contract between only two people, it has become a public, communal agreement, not merely a private decision expressive of individual autonomy. It is a form of social action, asserts Daniel Callahan, the director and co-founder of the Hastings Center and author, most recently, of *The Troubled Dream of Life*. It thus functions at the heart of this culture's social ethic, the glue which holds this diverse country and democratic experiment together. If PAS is legalized, it will dramatically alter the content of our public ethos, becoming part of the social framework of the citizens left behind.

In my father's final weeks, the family pitched in to be with him around the clock, attending to his needs, changing his sheets, feeding him ice. Undoubtedly he was experiencing pain at times, sometimes severely, though usually only temporarily. My father was also forced to endure some humiliation, being utterly dependent on either family or nurses to help with uncontrolled bodily discharges, for instance. During that time, echoing through my mind was the rhetoric I had heard in favor of PAS, usually wrapped in rights language: "We have a right to die with dignity." Such language seems to imply that pain or dependence on others robs us of dignity. In contrast, though, looking at my father, I did not feel that way. Yes, my dad experienced pain, so we tried desperately to find the right pain medication to help. And he was dependent on us, even to the point of being a burden on us. But the family would not have had it any other way. We genuinely felt and believed that mutual burden-sharing was part of what being a family was all about, and part of what being communal beings was about. Our respect for our father only increased through the difficult episode; at least in *our* minds he never lacked any dignity. On the contrary, his willingness to lean on our strength and compassion demonstrated a profound depth of character and inner grace.

Did my father lack dignity in his *own* mind? It is difficult to say, since he was rather noncommunicative in his final weeks. This much is clear, though: suicide for him simply was not a living option. It was not a category he thought in terms of, nor was it part of his intellectual furniture. At least one reason for that was this society's social ethic, which has not yet formally projected suicide as a legitimate response to a life deemed below an acceptable quality level. I could not help but watch my dad and wonder how it might have been different had suicide already become part of the intellectual framework and moral mentality of this society. When the pain was intense and his care increased, would he have considered himself obligated to request an earlier assisted death after seeing the strain that his dying put on the family? Would he have felt so burdensome that he felt obliged to hasten his own death?

## CONCLUDING THOUGHTS

Being witness to such a heartwrenching, anguishing experience as my father's death, I am reminded that to speak of issues of death, dying, and human suffering is a task that requires tremendous sensitivity and compassion. This is no mere academic exercise alone, but something vitally at the heart of the human condition, rife with human emotion and practical import. Though I sometimes fail, I attempt to tread this ground gingerly, hoping that my comments may resonate with both the intellectually honest and the emotionally sensitive, even if my readers do not entirely concur with my tentative conclusions or sympathize with my concerns.

This essay has attempted to carve out an important niche in the public debate for religiously motivated opponents of the practice of PAS, to call into question the widely assumed "right to die" of human beings and to make mention of some potential negative results of legalizing PAS. It has been my guiding premise that PAS and euthanasia are morally bankrupt and legally imprudent, and now I will offer a few additional reflections and provisional conclusions.

Rights language introduces many questions. Does such individualistic language underestimate the scope of its communal implications? Has such language extinguished categories like responsibility and virtue? Is it adequate to handle morally ambiguous cases like PAS? Does it often beg important prior questions like the prerogatives of human freedom and the essence of human nature? Does such language, as compelling as it may seem, merely skate on the surface of deeply philosophical, metaphysical, and moral issues?

The legalization of PAS would ensure that a significant shift takes place in the public attitude toward suicide. Logically, legally, and ethically, that would be the inevitable result. The ACLU, the organization fighting for PAS only with procedural safeguards in place, will be the same organization arguing tomorrow for the unconstitutionality of any safeguards they help institute today. If anyone doubts that, think for a moment how often the ACLU has helped the cause of any thoughtful regulation on abortion laws. Slippery slope arguments only constitute fallacies when the relationship between alleged causes and dramatic results is not clearly enough established. Concern over the consequences of legalizing PAS is well warranted, given the nature and content of such legislation. Regulatory guidelines would soon be seen as arbitrary, inviting covert evasion or blatant rejection, as the logic of PAS inexorably comes to fruition. As Christians we are being remiss when we do not express our strongest reservations about such an unwise and far-reaching law as PAS, which would be based on a relatively few truly "hard cases" that remind us that our best energies as a community are spent supporting the hospice movement, loving and supporting suffering patients and working toward even better pain control.

The laws of our democracy invariably reflect the moral convictions of the majority, whether the majority is right or wrong. If the echoes of public support for PAS reverberate into a mighty shout, the legislators are sure to hear and heed. PAS could very well become a salient feature of the social, economic, and political landscape of this society entering the twenty-first century: an expansive, decreasingly discriminatory, profit-driven enterprise offering suicide as one more "service" to be sought at a bargain. What might enhance the likelihood of this happening is Kevorkian's promise not to eat as long as he is imprisoned for breaking the new law. In effect, he argues, the state will then be assisting *his* suicide, and in that scenario he may well become something of a martyr and catalyst for the cause.

Meanwhile, the Christian Church should use its freedom to voice its concerns in a winsome and compelling manner, credibly and intelligently finding ways to influence the outcome of the public debate. Without claiming perfect discernment of God's will, we should willingly participate in discussing this dilemma, listening sensitively to those who disagree with us, becoming informed about the relevant issues to be addressed and questions to be asked and playing our own special part in the whole process. Lovers of God and humankind, committed to objective truth and normative morality, should not remain silent and uninvolved when they see their culture buy into the fleeting and misguided values of humanistic philosophy.

As the Church stresses its views on PAS, Christians should also remain insightfully aware of the need for harmony and integrity within and among all of their own various beliefs. Can Christians continue reconciling consistent opposition to PAS and euthanasia with inconsistent opposition to abortion or war? Can Christians justify opposing PAS if they support capital punishment? The earliest Christian communities were consistently "pro-life." They were pacifists who were firmly opposed to capital punishment, abortion, and suicide of any kind. Philosopher James Rachels's contention sounds reasonable that Christianity's eventual concession on issues like war and capital punishment, tempering its earlier radical stand, was but a politically expedient compromise, not something theologically and exegetically derived. Today Christians must be willing to think through their opposition to PAS, and to follow again their logic and convictions to their natural conclusions. I am convinced that the most logically and theologically consistent view for Christians opposed to the legalization of PAS is to be additionally opposed to war, capital punishment and abortion, though I know thoughtful Christians who disagree with me.

Assuming PAS is officially sanctioned here one day, then the Church will be faced with having to work on this issue more from the bottom up than from the top down, not unlike what has happened with abortion. What makes this appropriate is that being a Christian means not only that we believe rightly as individuals, but that we have been baptized into a community with a certain set of beliefs, practices, and morals, offering an alternative ethos to that of the world. It is relatively easy to stand against the legalization of abortion or euthanasia, and even to extol the virtues of the necessary sacrifices of bringing an unwanted pregnancy to term or of living until nature takes its course. But it is much more challenging, yet arguably closer to the heart of Christ, for the Church to reach out in love to the unwed mother or the suffering patient and provide for their needs to help them cope with their situations, so in desperation they do not resort to abortion or PAS. It is not the duty of the Church simply to engage in ethical debate and to battle laws against PAS, but to reach out to the suffering and needy, offering a cup of cold water and lending a sympathetic ear, to help convey a sense of meaning and impart a will to persevere to those who feel most like giving up.[13]

Notes
1.　In May 1993 the Michigan ban on assisted suicide was declared unconstitutional, largely for procedural reasons. In June 1993 that decision was reversed, restoring the ban, then subsequently reversed again. In December 1994 the Michigan State Supreme Court ruled that the ban was constitutional, and now that decision will likely be appealed to the United States Supreme Court. The state of Oregon recently became the first state to sanction a version of physician-assisted suicide, in the form of allowing doctors to give lethal prescriptions to terminally ill patients who fulfill certain criteria, such as coherently requesting such a prescription on numerous occasions.
2.　In *After Christendom?* (Nashville: Abingdon Press, 1991), Stanley Hauerwas contends that the reduction of religion to the realm of the personal is a politically motivated attempt to silence the Church.
3.　Richard John Neuhaus, *The Naked Public Square* (Grand Rapids: Eerdmans Publishing Co., 1984), p. 80.
4.　Ibid., p. 110.
5.　This is why the Michigan ban distinguished PAS from pain relief. The ban does not apply to "prescribing, dispensing, or administering medications or procedures if the intent is to relieve pain or discomfort and not to cause death even if the medication or procedure may hasten or increase the risk of death." One Michigan jury untrained in medical ethics and susceptible to the emotionally manipulative techniques used by Kevorkian's lawyer rendered a heretofore unprecedented decision in this regard, in essence, to apply the doctrine of double effect to PAS. They concluded that Kevorkian's assistance was primarily not meant to induce death but provide pain relief. What this seemingly innocuous decision implies is the bizarre conclusion that a lethal poison ought to be seen as a legitimate medical palliative.
6.　Thomas A. Mappes and Jane S. Zembaty, eds., *Social Ethics* (New York: McGraw-Hill Book Co., 1982), p. 50.
7.　Why I say it is only *generally* the case that following the moral rule results in the best consequences and is the right thing to do is because of the undeniable existence of exceptions to the rule. After all, Rahab lied about protecting Jewish spies and was rewarded for her faith, for example. But merely acknowledging occasional exceptional or extenuating circumstances does not deny the rule. That we feel obliged to legitimate an exception—and at times categorically reject certain forms of legitimation—goes to show our commitment to the rule. But it is not a Kantian form of commitment to a rule for its own sake, allowing for no possible exceptions. As Christians, though we affirm moral absolutes, we are convinced that they somehow flow out of

God's relational nature expressed throughout His creation. We worship a personal Christ and not merely abstract Reason, and we strive to be led by the Spirit of the Lawgiver, not just the letter of the law.

8.    Jerry Walls, *Hell: The Logic of Damnation* (Notre Dame: University of Notre Dame Press, 1992), p. 155. Walls argues for the moral connection between sin and human misery, writing that "to choose evil is to choose misery" and referring to the traditional Christian conviction that "it is impossible to further one's ultimate best interest by doing what is wrong, just as it is impossible to act against one's ultimate best interest by loving God and doing right."

9.    C. Everett Koop and Timothy Johnson, *Let's Talk: An Honest Conversation on Critical Issues* (Grand Rapids: Zondervan, 1992), p. 54.

10.   "A Reason to Die: Euthanasia Comes to Washington State," *Crisis* magazine, October 1991, p. 21.

11.   "The Return of Dr. Death," *Time* magazine, May 31, 1993, p. 38.

12.   Koop, *Let's Talk*, p. 46.

13.   My thanks to Neil Cowling, Elton Higgs, Stuart Noell, and Jerry Walls for their invaluable help with an earlier draft of this paper.

# THEOLOGICAL EDUCATION
# AFTER COMMUNISM: THE
# MIXED BLESSING OF
# WESTERN ASSISTANCE

MARK ELLIOTT

*This paper was delivered at the Consultation on Theological Education and Leadership Development in Post-Communist Europe, Oradea, Romania, 5 October 1994.*

In the summer of 1994 staff of St. Petersburg Christian University, which in fact is a seminary, sifted through literally tons of books donated from the West, ferreting out the occasional title relevant for a theological library. On the one hand, the task required time consuming sorting through mountains of boxes for the relatively rare gems in the rough. On the other hand, the shipping had been donated, several thousand useful titles were being gleaned from the heap, and seminarians would make use of a fair portion of the rest that the school would pass over. And so it is with Western assistance to theological education in the East, writ large: a mixed blessing. The question is: how help should and should not be given, and how help should and should not be received.

In February 1993 Overseas Council for Theological Education and Missions, Peter Deyneka Russian Ministries, and Wheaton College's Institute for East-West Christian Studies hosted a meeting of evangelical theological educators in Moscow. Insights drawn from that conference, plus seminary site visits and library research, served as the basis for a survey of the current state of Protestant theological education in the former Soviet Union. Three findings of that investigation follow.

*Mark Elliott is Professor of History and Director of the Institute for East-West Christian Studies, Billy Graham Center, at Wheaton College in Wheaton, Illinois.*

1. Prior to *glasnost* formal Protestant theological education was practically nonexistent. However, under Gorbachev an explosion of pent-up energy and demand saw well over 40 residential programs established in three years (1990-1992). These schools have emerged "in a manner unique in the history of Reformation churches. Never before, and nowhere else, have Protestants launched as many formal theological training programs as rapidly as they have in Soviet successor states."[1]

2. The new seminaries and training centers possess unusually dedicated staff and extraordinarily eager students, but the vast majority of the schools lack sufficient texts, adequate libraries, qualified faculty, and permanent facilities.

3. At the present time programs, representing several thousand residential students and several thousand additional extension and correspondence students, depend very heavily upon Western assistance. This third point serves as the focus of the present study.

How Western help is managed—or mismanaged—will make a major difference in the ability—or inability—of new schools to strengthen the Church in the East and to assist the Church as it seeks to witness to an enormous number of nonbelievers in its midst.

"We do not want ready-made Western Christianity to be dumped on us," a Russian theological educator reported in 1992. "We would love to have the tools, and then we will work it out for ourselves."[2] While such sentiments abound among post-Soviet bloc seminary administrators, paradoxically, Ralph Alexander of Biblical Education by Extension rightly characterizes the present fixation of these same leaders on Western accreditation as an "obsession."[3]

What does this readily observable striving for Western credentials portend and how might it foster rather than deter the manufacture of "ready-made Western Christianity" east of the old Iron Curtain? Russian church historian Walter Sawatsky has predicted that, particularly among evangelical Protestants, "the dominant literature in theology, and even the dominant theories for theological education will likely be drawn from North America," at the expense of training that is "contextually Slavic."[4] While the new Russian Protestant Euro-Asiatic Accreditation Association hosted a conference in October 1994 on the history of "The Protestant Movement in Russia" without Western participation, it appears, at the same time, that this body is likely to adopt wholesale Western criteria for the evaluation and credentialing of evangelical seminaries in the former Soviet Union.[5]

Western standards may be desirable in terms of required instructional facilities, faculty with earned doctorates, libraries of sufficient size and quality, and a broad curriculum. But for the foreseeable future such criteria are prohibitively expensive, beyond the reach of the vast majority of institutions in former Soviet bloc countries. Even worse, uncritical acceptance of Western standards, what Regent College professor Paul Stevens calls "slavish replication of Western curriculum and educational philosophy," would unquestionably doom theological education in former East bloc countries to abject economic dependence upon the West, and with it, *de facto* foreign control.[6]

Furthermore, to the extent that Western credentialing favors academic accomplish-ment over pastoral training and ministry, it may actually undermine, rather than facili-tate, Christian leadership training after communism. How so? If Western accreditation standards prevail, it quickly becomes apparent that at present the "right" credentials can only be had in the West, hence the scramble for study abroad, Western degrees, and what might be termed "bright flight."

Manfred Kohl's survey of theological educators in the East documented "overwhelm-ing support for training in-country."[7] But the decline in Soviet-style central church authority and the lure of the West already is spelling more and more post-Soviet seminar-ians opting for golden opportunities abroad. Borrowing from an American folk-song, "Will they ever return" or will they "ride forever 'neath the streets of Boston"? Past per-formance suggests another brain drain could be in the making. Seventy-five percent of Colombian theological students who have studied abroad never have gone home, the same for 85 percent of seminarians from the Caribbean and 90 percent of seminarians from India.[8] Is there any reason to believe it will be otherwise with former East bloc semi-narians?

Wilson Chow, president of Hong Kong's China Graduate School of Theology, just returned from the former Yugoslavia, already reports a "brain-drain of the theologically trained because of internal ethnic conflicts, the unstable political situation, [and] the attraction from seminaries in the West."[9] The present priority of North America's Association of Theological Schools upon globalization provides a perfect example of a Western academic standard being unhealthy and counterproductive for theological edu-cation elsewhere.[10] In the name of diversity and globalization too many Western seminar-ies currently are luring to their campuses rare, theologically trained seminary educators from abroad, often draining the lifeblood of struggling institutions. How ironic that Western seminaries could be so insensitive to the damage they may inflict upon schools outside the North Atlantic community—all in the name of a better understanding of the rest of the world!

Even if every theological student in the West did return home, unhealthy side effects still might cause the church in the East to question the advisability of study abroad. As Ralph Alexander points out, when seminarians study in another country, "training is removed from the normal ministry context."[11] In addition, seminarians' introduction to Western living standards and Western cultural values makes going home a difficult adjust-ment. The negative influences of narcissistic materialism and individualism are self evi-dent. But even defensible Western mores, such as the high premium placed on efficiency, productivity, and punctuality, pose problems for graduates attempting to re-enter societies that frequently value the building of relationships more highly than the completion of tasks by a set date. Also, modern higher criticism of the Scriptures, a staple of Western theological education—even in evangelical institutions reacting to it—will not be a wel-come import in the eyes of a great many church leaders east of the old Iron Curtain.[12]

The intense yearning of theological educators in the East for academic respectability actually could undermine effective leadership development. As Yugoslav theologian Peter Kuzmic argues, "We cannot uncritically copy Western models where truth is separated from practice and where the world of academia is separated from the world of ecclesia.

Instead of being accountable to the church, religious truth becomes a selfish, elitist, academic exercise."[13] In the same vein, theology professor Paul Stevens warns that "pride in degrees and publishing records" can lead to "the loss of humility as a Christian goal."[14] Both a respect for learning and a fear of learning—lest it replace a fear of the Lord—should stand side by side to prevent the one from breeding unbridled pride or the other from breeding mindless anti-intellectualism.

In the West programs exist which focus on the imparting of knowledge, or the formation of character, or practical and experiential preparation for ministry, or some combination of the three. Already in the East some of the same tendencies find expression. For example, the Evangelical Baptist Theological Seminary in Odessa appears to have the greatest emphasis upon academic scholarship of any Protestant institution in the former Soviet Union, while Donetsk Bible College stresses missions, ministry skills, and "experience-based learning with existing new churches."[15] At a February 1992 meeting on leadership training in Vienna, Austria, Greg Reader of International Teams stressed that "theological education should be accountable to the context it serves."[16] It would appear that an effective application of this principle may be observed at Donetsk: students maintain close, ongoing ties with local churches.

It can be argued that the lengthier and the more extensive theological education becomes, the greater the danger that it will increase the distance between pulpit and pew. Theological educators in the East should note that this "clergy-lay problem" requires conscious, ongoing, creative attention, and that the West is hardly the place to look for its solution.[17] (Ironically, the Kremlin's longstanding prohibition against Protestant theological education led to an *ad hoc* apprenticeship system of pastoral training, the unintended positive effect of which was to minimize the distance between clergy and laity.)

A final reason indiscriminate emulation of Western theological education would be unwise is that the West itself is increasingly unsure of the validity of its own approach, which one detractor has described as the "trained incapacity to deal with the real problems of actual living persons in their daily lives." Oddly enough, the world seems to crave this "desert experience...at the very moment when leaders in Western theological education are having serious misgivings about their enterprise."[18]

A seminary student studying in North America once asked, "How is it that the only form of theological education that has been given to us in Africa comes from the part of the world where the church is in decline?" An equally pointed rejoinder could have been, "How is it that, knowing the church in the West is in decline, African denominations are so hungry to get this sort of ministerial training that the West offers?"[19]

From a distance few can detect the disarray to be found in many Western churches and seminaries, especially through the rich camouflage of institutional endowments, bricks and mortar, and the flood of Christian books, videos, conferences, and the like. On the other hand, the global commitment and material prosperity of many Western evangelical churches, missions, and seminaries has translated into an extraordinary, perhaps unprecedented outpouring of assistance for fledgling seminaries and Bible institutes all across East Central Europe and the former Soviet Union. In most institutions Western assistance is welcome. The question is what kind of assistance is beneficial and who should make that decision.

If the case has been made that the Western connection to Christian leadership develop-ment in the East is a mixed blessing, what recommendations might contribute to more enlightened Western assistance?

1. Theological educators in East Central Europe and the former Soviet Union should be encouraged to develop culture-specific criteria for evaluating the effectiveness of leadership training programs. They should be creative and judicious in adapting, rather than submit-ting to the wholesale adoption of, Western accrediting standards. They should weigh care-fully the costs of accepting secular governments as the accrediting agents for theological schools. And they should look worldwide for innovative approaches to the evaluation of programs and graduates, such as those Jack Graves of Overseas Council for Theological Education has identified in Brazil and Indonesia.

2. They should have close institutional, faculty, and student interaction with the local church.[20] Churches do not exist in order to support seminaries. But seminaries should exist in order to support churches.

3. They should stress the importance of theological training in-country, for all the pre-viously discussed cultural, theological, and economic reasons. To that end seminaries in former Soviet bloc states should:

a. encourage study abroad only for especially talented, mature, and dedicated pas-tors targeted for teaching positions;

b. shorten the length of Western instruction, utilize extension programs and com-petency tests and encourage completion of M.A. programs, rather than longer M.Div. or doctoral programs;

c. encourage Western and indigenous churches, missions, and seminaries to work together in a few in-country advanced degree programs;

d. encourage Western partners to invest more resources in Western faculty teach-ing in the East, especially those with relevant language skills, and less in video talking heads and student scholarships for study in the West;[21]

e. also, before opting for West European or North American theological educa-tion, students from East Central Europe and the former Soviet Union should consider alternatives in non-Western nations that would entail much less cul-ture shock and theological dissonance, at a fraction of the cost. For example, the South Asia Institute of Advanced Christian Studies, Bangalore, India, would welcome students from East Central Europe and the former Soviet Union in its fully accredited programs for pastoral training or advanced degrees for future theological educators.[22]

4. Regarding curricula, Western theological educators would do well to encourage the introduction in former Soviet bloc evangelical institutions of:

a. courses on Eastern Orthodoxy and Catholicism which delineate common ground and insurmountable differences;[23] and

b. courses on biblical principles of conflict management. Unseemly strife abounds and demands serious attention within and between congregations, within and between denominations, within and between Christian confessions, and between Christians and persons of other faiths and no faith. Western Christian arbitration and conflict resolution services could be consulted for advice in developing instruction in this vital area.[24]

5. Above all, Evangelical Christians, East and West, must foster and practice greater cooperation, especially in so expensive and labor intensive an endeavor as theological education.[25]

## Notes

1.    Mark Elliott, "Protestant Theological Education in the Former Soviet Union," *International Bulletin of Missionary Research* 18 (January 1994): 19.

2.    Manfred Kohl, "Towards Globalization of Theological Education: Feasibility Study on Extending Theological Education into Eastern Europe and Parts of the Former USSR," thesis prospectus, Gordon-Conwell Theological Seminary, 15 (October 1992), appendix, p. 1.

3.    Ralph H. Alexander, "Assessment of Leadership in Post-Communist Europe," Consultation on Theological Education and Leadership Development in Post-Communist Europe, Oradea, Romania, 5 October 1994, pp. 3 and 5.

4.    Walter Sawatsky, "Visions in Conflict: Starting Anew Through the Prism of Leadership Training Efforts" in *Religion after Communism in Eastern Europe*, Niels Nielsen ed. (Boulder, CO: Westview Press, 1994), pp. 13, 20.

5.    Evro-Aziatskaya Akkreditatsionnaya Assotsiatsiya, "Protestantskoe dvizhenie v Rossii," pp. 13-15, October 1994, conference brochure.

6.    R. Paul Stevens, "Marketing Faith—A Reflection on the Importing and Exporting of Western Theological Education," *Crux* 28 (June 1992): 12. See also Alexander, "Assessment of Leadership," p. 4. For an Adventist exception to the dependency cycle, see Elliott, "Protestant Theological Education," p. 16.

7.    Kohl, "Towards Globalization," appendix, p. 1.

8.    Jack Graves, "Plugging the Theological Brain Drain," *Evangelical Missions Quarterly* 28 (April 1992): 155. See also "Bring Training In, Not People Out," *Albanian Insight*, 20 (27 February 1992): 2.

9.    Wilson Chow, "Theological Education: A Long and Hard Road," *China Graduate School of Theology Bulletin* (Winter 1993-94), p. 2.

10.   For the globalization emphasis see various theme issues on this subject in *Theological Education* (Spring and Autumn 1986; Spring and Autumn 1993; Autumn 1993 supplement); and Max L. Stackhouse, *Apologia: Contextualization, Globalization, and Mission in Theological Education* (Grand Rapids, MI: Eerdmans, 1988). For a brief overview see Robert J. Schreiter, "The ATS Globalization and Theological Education Project: Contextualization from a World Perspective," *Theological Education* 30 (Spring 1994): 81-88.

11.   Alexander, "Assessment of Leadership," p. 2.

12.   W. David Buschart, Kelvin G. Friebel, and Robert L. Webb, "'Faith and Horizons': Biblical and Theological Studies in Non-Western Contexts" (Regina, Saskatchewan: Canadian Theological Seminary for the Association of Theological Schools, 1993), pp. 5-6; Elliott, "Protestant Theological Education," p. 20.

13.   Peter Kuzmic, "Vision for Theological Education for Difficult Times," Theological Education Conference, Moscow, Russia, 12 February 1993, p. 5.

14.   Stevens, "Marketing Faith," p. 8.

15.   Sawatsky, "Visions in Conflict," p. 19.

16.   Author's notes, 5 February 1992.

17.  The Western mainline Protestant rendering of the dilemma and its cure reads as follows: in contrast to professionally trained clergy, laity in the West have remained at a "literalist, elementary school level in their religious understanding," which can only be corrected by means of a "rigorous educational process and post-Enlightenment tools of analysis and interpretation (historical, literary, social, psychological, philosophical)." Edward Farley, *The Fragility of Knowledge, Theological Education in the Church & the University* (Philadelphia: Fortress Press, 1988), pp. 92, 99. Evangelicals in the former Soviet Union and East Central Europe, who will regard such medicine as worse than the ailment, must ask themselves what they really want from the West. Paradoxically, the East could subject itself to Western mainstream theological education's childlike faith in the sanctity of objective analysis just when Western intellectuals increasingly debunk the possibility of detached empiricism.

18.  Stevens, "Marketing Faith," pp. 8 and 11. In 1983 Edward Farley (*Theologia: The Fragmentation and Unity of Theological Education* [Philadelphia: Fortress Press, 1983], pp. 19, 22) bemoaned the fragmentation of Western theological education, setting off what David Kelsey has described as "the most extensive debate in print about theological schooling that has ever been published" (*Between Athens and Berlin; The Theological Education Debate* [Grand Rapids, MI: Eerdmans, 1993], p. 1.). Torn between intellectual formation ("Berlin") and character and spiritual formation ("Athens"), between academic and professional preparation, between the theoretical and the practical, between head and heart, theological educators widely regard the lack of coherence in their enterprise as a given. (David H. Kelsey, *To Understand God Truly; What's Theological About a Theological School* [Louisville: Westminster/John Know Press, 1992], pp. 26, 105, 232-33.) That the discussants in the debate have been predominately white male theological faculty in North American mainline Protestant schools (Kelsey, *Between Athens and Berlin*, p. 2) has led to additional fissures along lines of gender and color. See The Mud Flower Collective, *God's Fierce Whimsy: Feminism and Theological Education* (New York: Pilgrim Press, 1985).

19.  Stevens, "Marketing Faith," pp. 7-8.

20.  Sawatsky, "Visions in Conflict," p. 12.

21.  Points a. through d. are abridged versions of comments in Elliott, "Protestant Theological Education," p. 16.

22.  "Introducing SAIACS." Contact: Dr. Graham Houghton, Principal, SAIACS, Box 7747, Kothanur P.O., Bangalore - 560077 India; tel: 0091-80-8465235; fax: 0091-80-5565547. The Norwegian Mission to the East is supporting seminarians from former Soviet bloc countries in India and the Philippines.

23.  Sawatsky, "Visions in Conflict," pp. 21-22.

24.  Western centers whose work in post-Soviet societies could be invaluable include the Mennonite Central Committee, Box 500, Akron, PA 17501; and the Institute for Christian Conciliation, 1537 Avenue D, Suite 352, Billings, MT 59102.

25.  Kuzmic, *Between Athens and Berlin*, pp. 10-11; Alexander, "Assessment of Leadership," p. 3. Perhaps the most successful cooperative effort to date to assist leadership training has been a Russian theological text project jointly administered by Overseas Council for Theological Education and Missions and Peter Deyneka Russian Ministries. By the end of 1994 it is projected that 400,000 volumes will have been published for some 7,000 residential and extension course students in the former Soviet Union. Jack Graves, "Former Soviet Union Theological Infrastructure Project, Textbook Development Component" (Greenwood, IN: Overseas Council for Theological Education and Missions, 1994).

# THE SOTERIOLOGICAL ORIENTATION OF JOHN WESLEY'S MINISTRY TO THE POOR

KENNETH J. COLLINS

The evidence pertaining to John Wesley's ministry to the poor in eighteenth-century Britain and Ireland is considerable. Indeed, reforming activities, of one form or other, were a part of the life of Methodism during its early days at Oxford, as well as the preoccupation of the seasoned Wesley.[1] Field preaching in the midst of coalminers, providing employment for the indigent, establishing lending stocks for the poor, and creating charity schools for the ignorant were a few of the many works of mercy undertaken by Wesley and the Methodists.

In the face of such evidence, the preliminary task of the historian must be to develop an appropriate hermeneutical framework which is best able to make sense not only of this rich diversity of activity, but which is also able to demonstrate the overarching motivation and purpose behind it. In a real sense, to address the theme of "Good News to the Poor" exclusively or almost exclusively along economic lines, as is often done today, is to make a judgment about the nature of Wesley's ministry to the poor which may belie not only its scope, but also its eighteenth-century context.[2] Two problems typically emerge from this approach: First, a predominantly economic reading of the "good news" to the poor often leaves the larger soteriological and valuational context of Wesley's ministry underdeveloped. In this setting such teleological questions as "Why did Wesley do what he did?" and "To what end did he do it?" are shunted aside in favor of the descriptive question "What did Wesley do?" Such an approach, then, often issues in a "flat" or "horizontal" reading of Wesley's reforming activity since it brackets out, to a significant degree, the depths of his specifically spiritual motivation.

*Kenneth J. Collins is the Samuel J. and Norma C. Womack Professor of Philosophy and Religion at the Methodist College in Fayetteville, N.C.*

Second, an overly economic reading, informed by contemporary political judgments, runs the risk of defining good and evil principally along economic or class lines where the sins of the oppressor, but not those of the oppressed, are clearly recognized.[3] Here the non-poor are not really a part of the environment where the redemptive activity of God takes place, though their continued presence is undoubtedly required if only to give added value, by way of contrast, to the poor. Indeed, the value-laden language of "preferential options" and the like, which have become a part of the rhetoric of liberation theology today, reveal the proper inclusions as well as exclusions—though in a way perhaps foreign to Wesley's own ethic.

In light of these two considerations, this present work will demonstrate that the soteriological orientation of Wesley's ministry to the poor is able to unite his multifarious reforms in terms of motivation, valuation, and purpose. To be sure, soteriology as a hermeneutical framework will not only be able to embrace the themes of economic justice—as in other approaches—but it will develop and evaluate such themes as part of a larger, more inclusive, whole.[4] Here all people, poor and non-poor, will be a part of the soteriological environment, though each group will undoubtedly play a different role. More importantly, here the love and worship of God, hardly a concern of modern economic theory, will be factored into the equation.

## I. IMPEDIMENTS TO MINISTRY: RICHES, IDOLATRY, AND LOVE OF THE WORLD

One of the difficulties of a work like E.P. Thompson's *The Making of the English Working Class* is its failure to realize sufficiently that not only were Wesley's economic categories, for the most part, medieval,[5] but that they were also, more importantly, soteriologically and ecclesiastically construed. For example, Wesley's definition of riches as "anything more than will procure the conveniences of life,"[6] as found in his sermon, "The Wisdom of God's Counsels" or his claim often repeated in his sermons that "one [who] has food and raiment sufficient for himself and his family, and something over, is rich,"[7] are judgments hardly reflected in any reputable economic theory, past or present. It is therefore all the more disturbing when contemporary Methodist interpreters of Wesley's economics ignore the ecclesiastical context of this definition and thereby render the transitions from church to state and from the eighteenth century to the twentieth that much easier, but also that much more dubious.

One of the clues, however, to Wesley's assessment of riches is found in his departure from the much-touted equation rich *equals* evil, an equation which has numerous modern variations. For although the Methodist leader's criticism of the rich was extensive, it was by no means total. To be sure, the preceding equation is undermined and its continuity broken in several places in Wesley's writings. For example, in his journal of 17 November 1759, Wesley notes, "It is well a few of the rich and noble are called." And he adds undoubtedly with hope and expectation, "Oh that God would increase their number!"[8] Second, in his piece, "The General Spread of the Gospel," produced in 1783, the Methodist evangelist exclaims: "Before the end even the rich shall enter into the kingdom of God."[9] Moreover, just a few years before his death, Wesley opined that "it is no more sinful to be rich than to be poor." But he immediately added, clarifying his meaning: "But it is dangerous beyond expression."[10]

What the preceding material from Wesley's writings suggests, then, is that the rich are neither evil by definition, nor do they constitute evil's irreducible core. In other words, the dividing line between good and evil does not by necessity run along economic lines, although it often does. Interestingly, Wesley held both of these ideas together, and in tension, and thereby preserved the basis for an even more radical assessment of human evil, one which moved beneath the realm of economics in order to probe the very depths of human desire and will, a substratum which, for Wesley at least, lay behind sinful social structures.

In substantiation of the foregoing claim, it should be noted that Wesley underscored the danger of riches, interestingly enough, not only by an appeal to economic considerations, but also by an appeal to the rhetoric of the heart. He did this in two key ways: First, riches were deemed exceedingly dangerous in that they strike at the very root of the personality and often displace the love of God with the love of the world. Indeed, riches as a temptation to idolatry, as a detraction from the glory of God, is a recurring theme in the sermon corpus.

Beyond this, Wesley stressed the danger of riches by means of a distinctive "Platonic" vocabulary—a vocabulary which reveals some of the more important value judgments made by this eighteenth-century leader. To illustrate, in this particular idiom believers are cautioned against setting their affections on "transient objects...things that fly as a shadow, that pass away like as a dream."[11] Wesley elaborates in his sermon "Walking by Sight and Walking by Faith," produced in 1788:

> I ask in the name of God by what standard do you judge of the value of things? By the visible or the invisible world? Bring the matter to an issue in a single instance: which do you judge best, that your son should be a pious cobbler or a profane lord.[12]

In fact, the members of the Methodist societies were enjoined repeatedly to lay up their treasures not on the earth but in heaven; to set their hearts not on penultimate things, but on that which is ultimate. "He who is a child of God can truly say," Wesley exclaims: "All my riches are above! All my treasure is thy love."[13] The first danger of riches, then, is that it strikes at the very heart of true religion: it magnifies the visible and discounts the invisible; it displaces, in other words, the love of God, and all holy affections, with the love of the world.[14]

Second, the danger of riches consists in their being a great hindrance to the love of neighbor. In other words, with the love of God despoiled, with the affections of the heart now turned towards temporal things and self will, it is impossible to love the neighbor as one ought. "A rich man may indeed love them that are of his own party, or his own opinion," Wesley observes, "but he cannot have pure, disinterested goodwill to every child of man. This can only spring from the love of God, which his great possessions expelled from his soul."[15] Again, riches intensify self-absorption and therefore beget and nourish "every temper that is contrary...to the love of neighbor,"[16] such tempers as contempt, resentment, revenge, anger, fretfulness, and peevishness.[17]

In considering the case of Methodism in particular, as a reflection of the universal Church, Wesley revealed the corrosive effect of riches in three movements. First, any revival of religion, like the evangelical revival of the eighteenth century, "must necessarily produce both industry and frugality."[18] That is, disciplined Christians will not only work assiduously, taking care to use wisely their talents and graces, but they will also cut off all needless expense. Second, these very characteristics, the fruit of vital religion, "cannot but produce riches."[19] Third, as riches increase, "so will pride, anger, and love of the world in all its branches," the very things which will vitiate the love of God and neighbor and thereby destroy vital religion. The movement has now come full circle.

## II. STEWARDSHIP AND THE PROMISE OF MINISTRY:
## THE LOVE OF GOD AND NEIGHBOR

One solution to the problem of undermining vital Christianity through riches is to maintain, as Theodore Jennings does, that the economic counsel of John Wesley as expressed in his well-known sermon, "The Use of Money" is seriously flawed and, therefore, must be rejected—at least in part.

To illustrate, Jennings, no doubt influenced by Marxist economic analysis, is apparently unwilling to grant Wesley the first two movements of his economic triad: namely, the advice to "gain all you can," and "save all you can."[20] Accordingly, for the phrase "gain all you can" Jennings substitutes something like "gain all you need." In other words, people should be allowed to earn no more than what they require for their basic human needs, regardless of the amount or difficulty of the work done. But observe that in his "Use of Money," Wesley does not restrict the *gaining* of money in terms of human need; instead, he maintains that a person's needs determine how much should be *given* to the poor. That is, to inhibit the gaining of money in a pre-emptive fashion may, in turn, restrict the amount of money available for ministry to the poor. In fact, what constraints Wesley does, after all, place on the rightful earning of money are in terms of such things as the health of laborers (they must neither hurt their bodies nor minds), and the well being of their neighbors (they must not hurt their neighbors in their bodies or their souls). Beyond this, Jennings is equally critical of Wesley's second counsel to "save all you can," since Wesley substantiates its value not by a specific appeal to the needs of the poor, but by an appeal to avoiding the "self-indulgence that leads to sin."[21]

The problem with Jennings' analysis, and others like it, is its failure to appreciate a truth readily acknowledged by Wesley, namely, that vital religion *necessarily* produces both industry (gain all you can) and thrift (save all you can), a point alluded to earlier. "For wherever true Christianity spreads," Wesley affirms, "it must cause diligence and frugality...."[22] In a similar fashion, Wesley admonishes the Methodists in his "Use of Money": "No more *sloth*! Whatsoever your hand findeth to do, do it with your might." And again: "No more waste! Cut off every expense which fashion, caprice, or flesh and blood demand."[23] Therefore, the prohibition or stifling of industry, the frustration or elimination of thrift by well-meaning social policy or by law may have, in the end, some unintended but nonetheless serious ramifications.

Fortunately, the solution which Wesley himself offered to the continuing problem of undermining Christianity through wealth was to add to the first two counsels a third, namely, "Give all you can."[24] Although this normative statement, this guide to behavior, is well known in Methodist circles, what has not been fully appreciated is the complex motivation which lay behind it. For example, in exhorting his own Methodist societies, Wesley actually made three distinct kinds of appeal by means of this prescription. First, and perhaps most important of all, he noted that believers should give all they can because it is the Lord who is the Creator and rightful Governor of the world. In other words, for Wesley, God is the true owner of all things; believers, therefore, are merely stewards of this bounty.

Second, for Wesley, the love of God through the discipline of stewardship must issue in the love of neighbor. Put another way, God has placed in the hands of those who have the necessities of life and something left over—Wesley's definition of rich— the wherewithal to minister to the poor. Therefore, the "rich" are to be the conduits, the channels, of the blessings of the Most High. "Let thy plenty supply thy neighbours' wants," Wesley urges in his sermon "On Worldly Folly."[25] Therefore, to stifle this gracious movement from God to humanity through needless self-indulgence is nothing less than robbing the poor. "Everything about thee which cost more than Christian duty required thee to lay out is the blood of the poor!"[26]

Third, Wesley acknowledged one last motivating factor, and it consisted, interestingly enough, in improving the spiritual life of those who ministered to the needy. Thus, in the larger economic and soteriological environment of ministry to the poor, there are three not two principal agents for Wesley: God and the poor, of course, but also those who served the poor. Indeed, Wesley's economic ethic is remarkably distinctive in that it expresses pastoral concern for the latter as well.

## III. JOHN WESLEY'S VARIEGATED MINISTRY TO THE POOR

Though seldom noticed, Wesley in his writings, especially in his sermon corpus, employs the term "the poor" in two key ways. First of all, commenting on Matthew 5:1-4, he specifically rejects a mere economic reading of the term "the poor" as found in "Happy are the poor in spirit for theirs is the kingdom of heaven."[27] Indeed, by means of this judgment, Wesley sought to reaffirm, once again and in a critical way, the radical nature of human evil which cannot be utterly identified with the particular sin of greed or with the acquisition of wealth. In fact, in his sermon "Upon Our Lord's Sermon on the Mount, Discourse the First," produced in 1748, the Methodist leader not only denies that the love of money is the root of all evil, but he also indicates something of the Lord's design in offering the Sermon on the Mount. Wesley writes:

> This sense [an economic reading] of the expression 'poor in spirit' will by no means suit our Lord's present design, which is to lay a general foundation whereon the whole fabric of Christianity may be built; a design which would be in no wise answered by guarding against one particular vice; so that even if this were supposed to be one part of his meaning, it could not possibly be the whole.[28]

The poor in spirit, then, the blessed of the Lord, are all those of whatever outward circumstances who "have that disposition of heart which is the first step to all real substantial happiness."[29] Poverty of spirit, in other words, entails lowliness in heart, and it begins "where a sense of guilt and of the wrath of God ends; and is a continual sense of our total dependence on him for every good thought or word or work."[30] In short, not outward circumstances but inward dispositions define this first definition of the poor, and, more importantly, these same dispositions constitute the general foundation of all true religion. But Wesley, quite obviously, also employed this term, secondly, in a largely economic way. To illustrate, in his sermon, "Dives and Lazarus," produced in 1788, Wesley exclaims:

> Hear this, all ye that are poor in this world. Ye that many times have not food to eat or raiment to put on; ye that have not a place where to lay your head, unless it be a cold garret, or a foul and damp cellar! Ye are now reduced to "solicit the cold hand of charity." Yet lift up your load; it shall not always be thus.[31]

Ever energetic in ministry, Wesley sought out those who lacked the necessities of life: he visited them in their homes and preached to them in the fields. As a result, he knew by firsthand experience how "devilishly false is that common objection, 'They are poor, only because they are idle.'"[32] Furthermore, Wesley's lifelong association with the destitute resulted in his love, respect, and appreciation for these children of God. In 1757, for instance, in a letter to Dorothy Furly, he exclaimed: "In most religious people there is so strange a mixture that I have seldom much confidence in them. I love the poor; in many of them I find pure, genuine grace, unmixed with paint, folly, and affection."[33] And a few years later, in 1765, Wesley once again demonstrated his affection for the impoverished and wrote in his journal: "I preached at Bath, but I had only the poor to hear, there being service at the same time in Lady H[untingdon]'s chapel. So I was just in my element."[34]

## A. The Temporal Needs of the Poor

So concerned was Wesley with the plight of the poor that he sought to improve their temporal condition through numerous ministries. Thus, in November 1740, for instance, Wesley undertook a humble experiment which involved about a dozen unemployed people, drawn from the Methodist societies, in the carding and spinning of cotton.[35] The next year, in 1741, greatly offended by the poverty within the United Society itself, Wesley developed a systematic program to feed the hungry, clothe the naked, employ the poor, and visit the sick.[36] In fact, according to Ward and Heitzenrater, for over forty years "all the class-money in London, amounting to several hundred pounds a year, was distributed to the poor by the stewards."[37] Moreover, these attempts to ameliorate the temporal condition of the needy, some more successful than others, were augmented in 1746 by the opening of a free dispensary to provide medical services[38] and by the institution of a lending-stock to offer cash to the impoverished. And though at its inception the stock did not amount to more than fifty pounds, it eventually served more than two hundred and fifty people.[39]

In light of the preceding material, it should be evident by now that a significant portion of Wesley's benevolent activity actually took place not indiscriminately but within the context of the Methodist societies themselves. In other words, lending stocks, dispensaries, collections and the like most often serviced those poor who were already participating in some way in the institutional life of Methodism.[40] More to the point, Wesley's sermons demonstrate a hierarchical order in meeting the temporal needs of the poor which clearly privileges those in the church over those beyond its walls. Thus, in assessing the proper distribution of goods beyond the real needs of one's family Wesley counsels: "If when this is done there be an overplus left, then 'do good to them that are of the household of faith.' If there be an overplus still, 'as you have opportunity, do good unto all men.' "[41] Not surprisingly, then, there are relatively few instances in either Wesley's Journal or his letters which chronicle acts of charity which are not somehow purposely related to a larger ecclesiastical and soteriological context.

Furthermore, Wesley's ever-present soteriological orientation is revealed not only in his concern over the temporal needs of the poor, but it is also demonstrated, once again, in his emphasis on the spiritual state of those who minister and in his critical assessment of their ministerial labors. To illustrate, in his homily, "Upon Our Lord's Sermon on the Mount, Discourse the Thirteenth," Wesley maintains that though believers may do good to their neighbors by dealing bread to the hungry and by covering the naked, they still may have "no part in the glory which shall be revealed."[42] And he displays the reasoning behind this judgment in the following excerpt from this same sermon: "For how far short is all this of that righteousness and true holiness which he has described therein! How widely distant from that inward kingdom of heaven, which is now opened in the believing soul!"[43]

Viewed from yet another perspective, Wesley affirms that before the love of God and neighbor is established in the heart through faith in Jesus Christ all works of piety and mercy are not good, technically speaking. And though the Methodist leader was obviously unwilling to call works of charity done apart from justifying faith good, strictly speaking, he was equally unwilling to call them "splendid sins" as some of his Calvinist friends were willing to do.[44] And, in a real sense, his doctrine of prevenient grace explains such reluctance. But perhaps the clearest expression of the indissoluble relationship between works of mercy and holy tempers is found in Wesley's sermon "On Charity" which was written in 1784. In this piece, for example, Wesley states: "That all those who are zealous of good works would put them in their proper place! Would not imagine they can supply the want of holy tempers, but take care that they may spring from them."[45]

So then Wesley endeavored to root his ministry to the poor not only in terms of a "horizontal axis," corresponding to the scope of the various temporal needs of the less fortunate, but also in terms of a "vertical axis" which plumbed the depths of motivation and purpose and thereby recognized the value of holy affections for those who ministered. Simply put, dispensing wealth improved the spiritual state of the giver as well as the temporal condition of the receiver. Hoarding wealth, on the other hand, spoiled the spiritual state of the rich and left the temporal needs of the poor neglected. In fact, in his *Notes on the New Testament* Wesley reveals a symbiotic relationship between the indigent and those who minister to them which operates under the larger providence of God. Commenting on the continuing existence of the poor in Matthew

26:11 "Ye have the poor always with you," Wesley exclaims, though perhaps some-what insensitively: "Such is the wise and gracious providence of God, that we may have always opportunities of relieving their wants, and so laying up for ourselves trea-sures in heaven."[46]

## B. The Spiritual Needs of the Poor

Though the descendants of the social gospel movement as well as some of the modern progenitors of liberation theology have, at times, looked askance at the lan-guage of "saving souls" as an instance of theological obscurantism, such language reverberates in the writings of John Wesley. At an early Methodist conference, for instance, Wesley asked those assembled to consider what is the office of a Christian minister? To which he and others replied: "To watch over souls, as he that must give an account."[47] And when he detailed the responsibilities of a "Helper" shortly there-after Wesley exclaimed, revealing much of his mission and purpose: "You have noth-ing to do but to save souls. Therefore spend and be spent in this work."[48]

To be sure, this particular emphasis of the redemption of souls, far from being an unusual or occasional one, continued throughout Wesley's life. Thus, in 1763, as he considered the purpose or end towards which the church should be directed, he wrote the following in his sermon "The Reformation of Manners":

> This is the original design of the church of Christ. It is a body of men compact-ed together in order, first, to save each his own soul, then to assist each other in working out their salvation, and afterwards, as far as in them lies, to save all men from present and future misery, to overturn the kingdom of Satan, and set up the kingdom of Christ.[49]

Moreover, when John wrote to his brother Charles in 1772, ostensibly to consider an aspect of the doctrine of Christian perfection, he reminded him, among other things, that his business as well as his own was "to save souls."[50]

In view of this emphasis, part of the good news to the poor according to Wesley consists not only in the transformation of the Christian community such that, with the holy tempers of love in place, the body of Christ is now impelled to share sacrifi-cially to meet the temporal needs of the poor, but it also consists in the glorious proclamation to the poor of the redemption of the inward person, that all people of whatever rank and station in life can be renewed in spirit, that the deepest recesses of the heart can be made anew. Indeed, in his sermon, "Salvation by Faith," preached at St. Mary's Oxford in 1738, Wesley points out that "whosoever believeth on him shall be saved,"[51] and, more importantly for the task at hand, he affirms in this same ser-mon that the poor themselves have a "peculiar right to have [this] gospel preached to them."[52]

This right to the gospel by the poor, however, is also matched by a need for the gospel in terms of both its temporal and spiritual aspects. In other words, just as Wesley was reluctant to draw an exact equation between the economic condition of the rich and their soteriological status, so too was he reluctant to draw a similar equa-tion in terms of the poor. That is, though the poor are often characterized by the graces of humility and patience, Wesley was well aware of the sins often peculiar to this estate. To illustrate, in an early manuscript sermon, Wesley asks the question, "O faith working by love, whither art thou fled"? To which he curtly replies: "among the wealthy? No. The 'deceitfulness of riches' there 'chokes the word...' Among the poor? No. 'The cares of the world' are there, 'so that it bringeth forth no fruit to perfection.' "[53] And much later, in 1784, the seasoned Wesley continued this theme and observed how "the poor were overwhelmed with worldly care, so that the seed they had received became unfruitful."[54] Beyond this, in his sermon "Spiritual Idolatry," Wesley affirms that idolatry in the form of "the desire of the flesh" plagues not only the rich, but the poor as well. "In this also 'the toe of the peasant...treads upon the heel of the courtier.' Thousands in low as well as in high life sacrifice to this idol."[55]

This leveling of all men and women as sinners, poor and non-poor, this universal flavor of sin, actually resulted in the enhanced status of the poor within the Methodist societies where rank and privilege, so valued by the world, counted for nothing. In fact, to know oneself as a sinner, to desire "to flee the wrath which is to come" was the only requirement for membership in a Methodist society—a characteristic of Methodist life, by the way, often resented by the rich.[56]

## C. Wesley's Valuation of Different Kinds of Ministry

One way of understanding the relation between holiness of heart and life and the works of mercy which flow from it, especially as such works relate to ministry to the poor, is found, once again, in the work of Theodore Jennings. Thus, for example, this contemporary scholar sets up a means/end relationship and maintains that the love of God reigning in the heart is a suitable means to works of charity and apparently to the-yet-higher end of reform of the political order. "Wesley emphasizes inward transformation," Jennings maintains, "because he is so earnestly interested in outward behavior."[57] Elsewhere in his writings, Jennings specifically links holiness to political goals, that is, to the elimination of private property and to the establishment of communism. "Wesley supposes that the Methodist movement will produce not only a spread of the gospel throughout the earth," he writes, "but also, and therefore, bring in the communist society."[58] And though these political goals themselves are questionable, especially in light of recent events in Eastern Europe, the valuational structure into which they are placed is even more dubious. Is the satisfaction of the temporal needs of the poor, though important, the very highest goal, the telos, at which Wesley aimed? Was political transformation really the end, the major purpose of the eighteenth-century revival? Or is this modern reading of Wesley, in its attempt to be relevant, actually reductionistic in that it entails the substitution of the penultimate for what is truly ultimate?

Yet another way of reading Wesley, of construing the relationship between the love of God reigning in the heart and all manner of good works (individual, political, social) is to contend that the one endlessly leads to the other in a cyclical fashion. In other words, in this interpretation, the love of God and neighbor issues in works of mercy which in turn enhance the love of God and neighbor.[59] Here each element is a means to the other and the question of valuation, of an ultimate telos, is thereby avoided.

Though this second reading of Wesley is much more plausible than the first, it too must be judged as inadequate simply because it cannot incorporate the kinds of value judgments which Wesley did, after all, make in this area. For example, in his sermon, "On Visiting the Sick," produced in 1786, Wesley advises his visitors in the following fashion:

> But it may not be amiss usually to begin with inquiring into their outward condition. You may ask whether they have the necessaries of life. Whether they have sufficient food and raiment. If the weather be cold, whether they have fuel.[60]

But after this, Wesley asserts, the visitor is to proceed to things of *greater* value. "These little labours of love," he writes, "will pave your way to things of greater importance. Having shown that you [have] a regard for their bodies, you may proceed to inquire concerning their souls."[61] Furthermore, Wesley repeats this judgment, no doubt for emphasis, but this time he clearly displays what is the *telos* of all ministry: "While you are eyes to the blind and feet to the lame, a husband to the widow and a father to the fatherless, see that you still keep *a higher end in view*, even the saving of souls from death, and that you labour to make all you say and do subservient *to that great end*."[62]

Though these value judgments have seldom surfaced in the secondary literature, they are by no means idiosyncratic but represent Wesley's own thinking throughout his career. For example, much earlier, in 1748, Wesley had written concerning those engaged in ministry that "He doth good, to the uttermost of his power, even to the bodies of men.... How much more does he rejoice if he can do any good to the soul of any man!"[63] And two years later Wesley continued this theme in his sermon "Upon Our Lord's Sermon on the Mount, Discourse the Thirteenth" and wrote:

> Over and above all this, are you zealous of good works? Do you, as you have time, do good to all men? Do you feed the hungry and clothe the naked, and visit the fatherless and widow in their affliction? Do you visit those that are sick? Relieve them that are in prison? Is any a stranger and you take him in? Friend, *come up higher*.... Does he enable you to bring sinners from darkness to light, from the power of Satan unto God?[64]

Two points are noteworthy in light of the preceding evidence: first, for Wesley at least, a part of what it means to love your neighbor as yourself always involves the exercise of both material gifts and spiritual talents; it entails the employment of all those gifts and graces which will enhance the physical well being of the poor *and* their spiritual character. Second, and perhaps more importantly, though the material needs of the neighbor have chronological priority; they clearly do not have valuational priority in Wesley's thought,[65] for their fulfillment prepares the way, to use Wesley's own terminology, for things of *greater importance*.

But perhaps the most lucid expression of the goal of ministry as well as of its accompanying motivating factors in terms of the value and necessity of personal inward transformation (spirituality) is found in the following selection from the sermon *On Zeal*, a sermon which epitomizes Wesley's thought in this area and which provides insight into his ethical motivation and concern. Notice, for instance, what is at the heart of this ethic and the consequences which flow from it. Wesley declares:

> In a Christian believer *love* sits upon the throne, which is erected in the inmost soul; namely, love of God and man, which fills the whole heart, and reigns without a rival. In a circle near the throne are all *holy tempers*: long-suffering, gentleness, meekness, goodness, fidelity, temperance—and if any other is comprised in "the mind which was in Christ Jesus." In an exterior circle are all the *works of mercy*, whether to the souls or bodies of men. By these we exercise all holy tempers; by these we continually improve them, so that all these are real *means of grace*, although this is not commonly adverted to. Next to these are those that are usually termed *works of piety*: reading and hearing the Word, public, family, private prayer, receiving the Lord's Supper, fasting or abstinence. Lastly, that his followers may the more effectually provoke one another to love, holy tempers, and good works, our blessed Lord has united them together in one—the *church*, dispersed all over the earth; a little emblem of which, of the church universal, we have in every particular Christian congregation.[66]

In this sermon, then, it is as if Wesley has allowed us to peek into the throne room of his entire theological and moral enterprise.[67] And on the throne sits not any political ideology nor works of mercy, however noble or valuable they may be. No, love itself sits on the throne, and next to it are all those holy tempers (holiness) described earlier. And it is precisely only when these elements are in place, as both motivating factors *and* as the highest goal of all ministry, that Wesley is then willing to consider works of mercy, piety and the like. As noted earlier, "No outward works are acceptable to him [God] unless they spring from *holy tempers*,"[68] he cautions. And again, "That all those who are zealous of good works would put them in their proper place! Would not imagine they can supply the want of holy tempers, but take care that they may spring from them!"[69] Therefore all those "dispositions of mind" like meekness, gentleness and long-suffering, etc., are not beside the point, a pious extravagance or indulgence, but are "absolutely necessary...for the enjoyment of present or future holiness."[70] Indeed, they are nothing less than the lodestars of the moral life, the key to Wesley's ethic.

## CONCLUSION

It should be apparent by now that the soteriological orientation of John Wesley's ministry to the poor is marked by three carefully drawn axes. First, Wesley's horizontal axis of ministry, directed towards the temporal needs of humanity, is more broadly conceived than some and includes the principal agents of God, the poor, as well as those who are engaged in service. Second, Wesley's vertical axis of ministry is attentive not only to the proper spiritual motivation of those who minister to the poor, underscoring the crucial nature of right tempers, but it is also attentive to the spiritual life of the poor themselves. Indeed, for Wesley, all people, poor and non-poor, young and old, male and female, need to be renewed through faith in love. Third, the

Methodist leader's valuational axis, present in several of his later sermons, not only assesses the worth of temporal and spiritual ministry, but it also places nothing other than holy love at the center of things in terms of both motivation and purpose. Next in importance, of course, are all those holy tempers of the human heart from which flow works of mercy and works of piety. Indeed, for Wesley, only when this "inward" work has begun is one ready for vigorous, redemptive service.

Viewed from another perspective, these three axes demonstrate the truly radical nature of John Wesley's ministry to the poor in that he realized that the evils of economic injustice, though significant, were informed by more basic evils which had their roots in the human heart. Accordingly, the greed of the rich, their taste for luxury and waste, could not be overcome simply by state fiat, nor by moralizing, but by a transformation of the inward person as well.

Moreover, with respect to the poor themselves, Wesley was critical enough to realize that no group or class has a privileged soteriological status since all have fallen short of the glory of God. Indeed, it was precisely on this basis of a universal need for redemption, of a radical transformation of the human heart, that Wesley was able to break out of the political strife and animosity so typical of his day to bring together the poor and those who ministered to them in a larger, more inclusive circle of ministry, to foster mutual concern and affection among them as joint members of the body of Christ, and ultimately to unite them in the broadest circle of love.

Notes

1.    Many of the works of charity undertaken by the early Methodists are described in considerable detail in Henry D. Rack, *Reasonable Enthusiast: John Wesley and the Rise of Methodism* (Philadelphia: Trinity Press International, 1989), p. 361.

2.    For an example of a treatise which discusses "Good News to the Poor" principally in economic terms cf. Theodore W. Jennings, Jr., *Good News to the Poor: John Wesley's Evangelical Economics* (Nashville: Abingdon Press, 1990). It is an interesting exercise, however, to check the references to Wesley's writings in this work. What one finds is that Jennings often cuts off the quotation at a suitable point in order to favor a particular reading of the text and also in order to eliminate its larger soteriological context. For example, in citing Wesley's letter to Freeborn Garrettson in September 1786, Jennings writes: "Most of those in England who have riches love money, even the Methodists—at least, those who are called so. The poor are the Christians. I am quite out of conceit with almost all those who have this world's goods." Unfortunately, Jennings omits the following two lines—perhaps he was fearful of an otherworldly interpretation—which are a vital clue to the meaning of this passage: "Let us take care to lay up our treasure in heaven. Peace be with your spirit." Cf. John Telford, ed., *The Letters of John Wesley, A.M.*, 8 vols. (London: The Epworth Press, 1931), 7:343-44.

3.    The great danger in defining evil along class lines is the tendency to consider "the other" as the epitome of evil. In fact, Elsa Tamez writes that the redeemed poor now have "the ability to distinguish between life and death. We can identify those who produce death, the principalities and powers that govern the earth, the anti-Christs." Cf. Elsa Tamez, "Wesley as Read by the Poor," in *The Future of the Methodist Theological Traditions*, M. Douglas Meeks, ed. (Nashville: Abingdon Press, 1985), p. 80.

4.    Note that in Wesley's commentary on Luke 4:18 ("The Spirit of the Lord is upon me,

because he hath anointed me to preach the Gospel [good news] to the poor...) he conceives the phrase, by his own admission, both literally *and* spiritually. Cf. John Wesley, *Explanatory Notes Upon the New Testament* (Salem, Ohio: Schmul Publishers), p. 151.

5.   Robert C. Haywood, "Was John Wesley a Political Economist?" *Church History* 33 (September 1964): 314-321.

6.   Albert C. Outler, ed., *The Works of John Wesley*, vols. 1-4. *The Sermons* (Nashville: Abingdon Press, 1984), 2:560. The "exceptions" which Wesley allows to the rule of not laying up treasure on earth are found in his sermon "Upon the Lord's Sermon on the Mount, Discourse, VIII" where he states: "Lastly, we are not forbidden in these words to lay up from time to time what is needful...in such a measure as, first, to 'owe no man anything'; secondly, to procure for ourselves the necessaries of life; and thirdly, to furnish those of our own house with them while we love and with the means of procuring them when we are gone to God." Cf. Outler, *Sermons*, 1:619. ("Upon Our Lord's Sermon on the Mount," VIII)

7.   Outler, *Sermons*, 3:520. ("On Riches") Bracketed material is mine. For similar definitions of riches cf. Outler, *Sermons*, 3:230, 3:237, 3:520, and 4:179.

8.   Ibid., 4:358. ("The One Thing Needful")

9.   Ibid., 2:494. ("The General Spread of the Gospel") It is interesting to note that in this sermon the very last to enter the kingdom of God are not the rich, but "the wise and learned, the men of genius, the philosophers...."

10.   Ibid., 4:11. ("Dives and Lazarus")

11.   Ibid., 4:56. ("Walking by Sight and Walking by Faith") For Wesley, one of the tests which would determine the state of the heart, whether God is indeed its highest love, is revealed in the following admonition: "Unless thou givest a full tenth of thy substance, of thy fixed and occasional income, thou dost undoubtedly set thy heart upon thy gold, and it will 'eat thy flesh as fire.' " Cf. "The Danger of Increasing Riches" in Outler, *Sermons*, 4:181.

12.   Ibid., 4:56 ("Walking by Sight and Walking by Faith")

13.   Ibid., 4:137-138. ("On Worldly Folly")

14.   Wesley again indicates the malign effect of riches on the soul in his piece "Upon the Lord's Sermon on the Mount, VIII" where he writes, "You have murdered your own soul. You have extinguished the last spark of spiritual life therein. Now indeed, in the midst of life you are in death. You are a living man, but a dead Christian. 'For where your treasure is, there will your heart be also.' " Cf. Outler, *Sermons*, 1:620.

15.   Ibid., 3:522 ("On Riches") Leslie Church and Leon Hynson maintain that the love of God, from which flows the love of neighbor, is the key to Wesley's ethics, both personal and social. In fact, the former contends that the early Methodists were actually philanthropists rather than social reformers. Cf. Leslie F. Church, *More About the Early Methodist People* (London: Epworth Press, 1949), p. 207ff. and Leon Hynson, *To Reform the Nation* (Grand Rapids, Michigan: Francis Asbury Press, 1984), pp. 93-106.

16.   Outler, *Sermons*, 3:526. ("On Riches")

17.   Ibid. ("On Riches")

18.   Rupert E. Davies, *The Works of John Wesley*, vol 9. *The Methodist Societies: History, Nature, and Design* (Nashville: Abingdon Press, 1989), p. 529. For a detailed examination of Wesley's economic ethics and their relation to piety and spirituality cf. Wellman J. Warner, *The Wesleyan Movement in the Industrial Revolution* (New York: Russell and Russell, 1967), pp. 165-187.

19.   Warner, *The Wesleyan Movement*, pp. 165-184. Though Wesley clearly rejected what the twentieth century has termed "the gospel of wealth," he nevertheless strongly associated vital religion and the specter of riches as detailed above. However, his statement that industry and frugality will necessarily produce wealth is dependent on the assumption that one lives in a rich country at the start. Indeed, no amount of industry and frugality on the part of the poor ("save

all you can; gain all you can") will ever produce riches in some of the poorest countries today.

20. Jennings, *Good News*, p. 166-67. For a view which maintains that Wesley's rules on the use of money are no longer applicable in modern, industrial societies cf. Charles M. Elliot, "The Ideal of Economic Growth," in *Land, Labour and Population in the Industrial Revolution*, E.L. Jones and G.E. Mingay, eds. (Edward Arnold Publishers, 1967), p. 75-99.

21. Jennings, *Good News*, p. 167.

22. Outler, *Sermons*, 4:95-96 ("Causes of the Inefficacy of Christianity") Emphasis is mine. For Wesley, "giving all you can" was to be voluntary, uncoerced. Indeed, the Oxonian feared that legislation in this area, either by the church or by the state, would remove not only freedom, civil liberty in particular, but also the element of worship in such gracious ministry. For example, in a letter to Miss March in 1776, Wesley writes: "It is impossible to lay down any general rules, as to 'saving all we can' and 'giving all we can.' In this, it seems, we must needs be directed from time to time by the unction of the Holy One." Cf. Telford, *The Letters of John Wesley*, 6:207.

23. Outler, *Sermons*, 2:279. ("The Use of Money")

24. Ibid., 2:277. ("The Use of Money")

25. Ibid., 4:133-34. ("On Worldly Folly")

26. Ibid., 3:255. ("On Dress") Rack cautions contemporary interpreters of Wesley's economic ethics that "the category of 'the poor' in the eighteenth century is itself an imprecise term.... The poor that Wesley begged for in times of distress were often tradesmen down on their luck." Cf. Rack, *Reasonable Enthusiast*, p. 441.

27. Wesley, *Explanatory Notes Upon the New Testament*, p. 19.

28. Outler, *Sermons*, 1:476-477. ("Upon Our Lord's Sermon on the Mount, I") Bracketed material is mine.

29. Ibid., 1:476. ("Upon Our Lord's Sermon on the Mount, I") Nevertheless, Wesley did not always keep his two definitions of the poor apart. At times, for example, he conflated them and identified the qualities of the poor in spirit, like humility and gentleness, with the penniless. And, on the other hand, he associated pride—the opposite of poverty of spirit—with the rich. "O what an advantage have the poor over the rich!" the Methodist leader writes. "These are not wise in their own eyes, but all receive with meekness the ingrafted word which is able to save their souls." Cf. Nehemiah Curnock, ed., *The Journal of the Rev. John Wesley, A.M.*, 8 vols. (London: The Epworth Press, 1938), 7:436.

30. Outler, *Sermons*, 1:482. ("Upon Our Lord's Sermon on the Mount, Discourse I")

31. Ibid., 4:13 ("Dives and Lazarus") Some of the descriptions of the poor, found in Wesley's sermons, are no doubt problematic for the modern reader. For example, in his "Upon Our Lord's Sermon on the Mount, Discourse the Eleventh," Wesley states: "Nor does this [the way to perdition] only concern the vulgar herd, the poor, base, stupid part of mankind." However, see Outler's comment (number 20) found on page 667, volume one of the *Sermons*.

32. Reginald W. Ward, and Richard P. Heitzenrater, eds., *The Works of John Wesley, vol. 20. Journals and Diaries I* (Nashville: Abingdon Press, 1991), p. 445. Moreover, Wesley criticized the insensitivity of Juvenal, who in his ignorance concerning poverty, declared: *"Nil habet infelix paupertas durius in se: quam quod ridiculos homines facit!"* Cf. Outler, *Sermons*, 2:227.

33. Telford, *The Letters of John Wesley*, 3:229.

34. Curnock, *The Journal*, 5:148-149.

35. Ward and Heitzenrater, *The Works of John Wesley*, 19:173.

36. Ibid., 19:193-94. For an assessment of Wesley's social ministries from a third-world perspective cf. Aubin de Gruchy, "Beyond Intention—John Wesley's Intentional and Unintentional Socio-economic Influences on 18th Century England," *Journal of Theology for Southern Africa* 68 (Spring 1989): 75-85.

37. Ward and Heitzenrater, *The Works of John Wesley*, 20:176, note number 45.

38. Marquardt points out the need for this benevolent activity and writes: "*Eine weitere wirk-same Hilfe neben der Versorgung mit Lebensmitteln und Lieidung brachte eine andere Massnahme, die Wesley 1746/47 in London und Bristol eingeleitet hatte: die medizinische Versorgung der Armen. Der hygienische Zustand vieler Unterfünfte war katastrophal, die medizinische Versorgung völlig unzureichend, die Ernahrung oft schlect und die Kenntnisse in bezug auf Lebensweise und Krankenpflege waren minimal....*" Cf. Manfred Marquardt, *Praxis und Prinzipien der Sozialethik John Wesleys* (Gottingen: Vandenhoeck & Ruprecht, 1977), p. 26-27.

39. Ward and Heitzenrater, *The Works of John Wesley*, 20:125. One of the reasons for the efficiency of this stock was that Wesley laid down a number of ground rules: first, only twenty shillings was to be lent at a time; second, this sum was to be repaid weekly within a three-month period. Cf. Ward and Heitzenrater, *The Works of John Wesley*, 20:204.

40. It should be noticed that the leading motif which informs Wesley's concept of justice is not equality but "the rendering to each his or her due," as found, for instance, in the writings of Plato, Cicero, and other classical authors. Holland and Howell who, quite perceptively, note this difference write: "Wesley's definition of the 'just' is Ciceronian, connoting rendering to all 'their due' and prescribing 'exactly what is right, precisely what ought to be done,' said, or thought, both with regard to the Author of our being, with regard to ourselves, and with regard to every creature which he has made." Cf. Lynwood M. Holland and Ronald F. Howell, "John Wesley's Concept of Religious and Political Authority," *Journal of Church and State* 6 (Autumn 1964): 301.

41. Outler, *Sermons*, 2:277. ("The Use of Money")

42. Ibid., 1:689-690. ("Upon Our Lord's Sermon on the Mount, Discourse the Thirteenth")

43. Ibid., 1:690. ("Upon Our Lord's Sermon on the Mount, Discourse the Thirteenth"). Vilem Schneeberger affirms that Wesley's benevolent activities grew out of soteriological considerations, that is, the love of neighbor is nothing less than the outworking of vital faith. Cf. Vilem Schneeberger, *Theologische Wurzeln des sozialen Akzents bei John Wesley* (Zurich and Stuttgart: Gotthelf Verlag, 1974).

44. For instance, in his sermon, "The Reward of Righteousness," Wesley writes: "when you visit them that are sick, or in prison—these are not 'splendid sins,' as one marvelously calls them, but 'sacrifices' wherewith God is well pleased." Cf. Outler, *Sermons*, 3:404.

45. Ibid., 3:305. ("On Charity") Bett affirms that Wesley strongly associated good works and the love of God simply because "there is no real love of our fellows that does not ultimately spring from the love of God, shed abroad in our hearts by the Holy Spirit." Cf. Henry Bett, *The Spirit of Methodism* (London: The Epworth Press, 1937), p. 200.

46. Wesley, *Explanatory Notes Upon the New Testament*, p. 86.

47. Thomas Jackson, ed., *The Works of John Wesley*, 14 vols. (Grand Rapids, Michigan: Baker Book House, 1978), 8:309.

48. Ibid., p. 310.

49. Outler, *Sermons*, 2:302. ("The Reformation of Manners") In addition, in his "Letter to a Clergyman" Wesley writes: "I think he is a true, evangelical Minister, *diakonos*, "servant" of Christ and his church, who…"so ministers," as to save souls from death, to reclaim sinners from their sins;…" Cf. Jackson, *Works*, 8:498.

50. Telford, *The Letters of John Wesley* , 5:316. More than a decade later, in 1784 to be exact, John reminisced about the founding of Methodism and the employment of lay preachers and exclaimed: "He chose a few young, poor, ignorant men, without experience, learning, or art; …seeking no honour, no profit, no pleasure, no ease, but merely to save souls." Cf. Outler, *Sermons*, 2:558-559.

51. Outler, *Sermons*, 1:128. ("Salvation by Faith")

52. Ibid. ("Salvation by Faith") Bracketed material is mine.

53. Ibid., 3:536. ("The Trouble and Rest of Good Men") Manuscript sermons are those which,

for whatever reason, Wesley saw fit not to publish, although he did keep copies of them among his papers. Interestingly, all these pieces were written early, relatively speaking, and range from 1725 to 1741. Among the manuscript sermons are such important works as "The Image of God," and "The One Thing Needful." See Outler's introduction to his critical edition of Wesley's sermons for more on this particular genre.

54. Ibid., 2:565. ("The Wisdom of God's Counsels")

55. Ibid., 3:106. ("Spiritual Idolatry") Wesley also tried to comfort poor believers by directing their attention to the providence of God. In his Journal on 31 December 1772 Wesley wrote "Being greatly embarrassed by the necessities of the poor, we spread all our wants before God in solemn prayer; believing that He would sooner 'make windows in heaven' than suffer His truth to fail." Cf. Curnock, *Journal,* 5:495.

56. In his sermon, "On Riches," for instance, Wesley points out the contempt which the rich often hold towards their "inferiors," and in his "On the Danger of Riches" he underscores the reluctance of the wealthy even to be among the poor. Cf. Outler, *Sermons,* 3:108 and 3:244.

57. Jennings, *Good News,* p. 144.

58. Theodore W. Jennings, Jr., "Wesley's Preferential Option for the Poor," *Quarterly Review* vol. 9, no. 3 (Fall 1989): 22. Ignoring the political and social context of eighteenth-century England, Jennings contends that Wesley repudiated the right of private property. However, there is sufficient evidence in Wesley's own writings to demonstrate that he upheld both religious and civil liberty. More to the point, in his "Thoughts upon Liberty" Wesley observes that civil liberty entails "a liberty to enjoy our lives and fortunes in our own way; to use our property, whatever is legally our own, according to our own choice." And in his "Observations on Liberty" he adds: "Civil liberty is a liberty to dispose of our lives, persons, and fortunes, according to our own choice, and the laws of our country." Cf. Jackson, *Works,* 11:41, 11:92.

59. Wesley maintained that works of piety as well as works of mercy are in some sense necessary to sanctification. In other words, if there be time and opportunity, these works are the normal means to an improvement of the rich grace of God. Wesley, however, did not contend that doing good works necessarily results in an increase in holiness. The emphasis here, as elsewhere, is on the grace of God and works of mercy as a means of that grace. Cf. Outler, *Sermons,* 2:164. ("The Scripture Way of Salvation")

60. Ibid., 3:390. ("On Visiting the Sick")

61. Ibid., p. 391. ("On Visiting the Sick") These hortatory comments found in the sermons reveal that in his ministry to the poor Wesley was never simply preoccupied with their temporal needs, important though they were, but he also was ever concerned with the transcendent, with the issues of God and eternity, a trait which gave his economic ethic, at least at times, a decidedly "other worldly" emphasis. "Every pound you put into the earthly bank is sunk," Wesley writes in his "The More Excellent Way," "it brings no interest above. But every pound you give to the poor is put into the bank of heaven." Cf. Outler, *Sermons,* 3:276.

62. Ibid., 3:393. ("On Visiting the Sick") Emphasis is mine.

63. Ibid., 1:519. ("Upon Our Lord's Sermon on the Mount, Discourse the Third") With respect to the roles of ministry, the task of visiting the sick (and the poor) demonstrates not separation as in some praxis models, not ministry which occurs in one direction only, from the poor to those who minister to them, but it reveals, once again, a mutuality of need and of love in an ever larger circle of ministry. Moreover, this mutuality of need and love is amply displayed in Wesley's sermon, "On Visiting the Sick," in which he counsels his readers to visit the afflicted *in person* for two principal reasons: first, unlike a physician, the visitor can do great good to the souls of men and women. Second, sending relief by another likewise does not improve one's own graces; there is no advance, in other words, in the love of God and neighbor. "You could not gain that increase in lowliness, in patience, in tenderness of spirit, in sympathy with the

afflicted," Wesley notes, "which you might have gained if you had assisted them in person." Cf. Outler, *Sermons*, 3:389, 393.

64. Ibid., 1:695. ("Upon Our Lord's Sermon on the Mount, Discourse the Thirteenth") Emphasis is mine.

65. Ibid. ("Upon Our Lord's Sermon on the Mount, Discourse the Thirteenth")

66. Ibid., 3:313-14. ("On Zeal")

67. Though there is no evidence that Wesley ever read St. Teresa of Avila's *Interior Castle*, the central images which both spiritual leaders use to describe the Christian life are remarkably similar. Both, for instance, employ paradigmatic metaphors which not only contain implicit value judgments, but they also highlight the crucial nature of love. For example, Teresa's seventh mansion and its "geographical" location in the center of the castle is analogous to Wesley's placing of love on the throne from which all else in the Christian life flows. Compare Teresa of Avila, *Interior Castle*, trans. E. Allison Peers (New York: Doubleday, 1989), p. 206ff with Outler, *Sermons*, 3:313-14. ("On Zeal").

68. Outler, *Sermons*, 3:320. ("On Zeal") Bracketed material is mine.

69. Ibid., 3:305. ("On Charity")

70. Ibid., 4:223. ("On Living Without God") The danger of beginning not with love and holy tempers but with political and economic concerns is that "justice" so conceived will most likely be unreformed, speckled with anger, class animosity, and perhaps even outright hatred of the middle-class or the rich. In other words, its concern for the poor will be expressed in all those unholy tempers against which Wesley inveighed. Once again, love and holiness are the proper starting point. Only then will the poor be properly ministered to and receive the justice they deserve.

# BOOK REVIEWS

Pelikan, Jaroslav, *Christianity and Classical Culture. The Metamorphosis of Natural Theology in the Christian Encounter with Hellenism* (Gifford Lectures at Aberdeen, 1992-1993). New Haven, London: Yale University Press, 1993. xvi, 368 pps. ISBN 0-300-05554-4.

Based on the Gifford lectures given at the University of Aberdeen in 1992 and 1993, Pelikan's book is a significant contribution to understanding the fourth Christian century and the influence of decisions made during that period upon subsequent generations of Christian theologians. The driving questions which gave form to the lectures and the subsequent volume related to the interaction of Christian ideas and Classical Greek culture; the case studies chosen for investigation were the four theologians known as "the Cappadocians" according to their home province: Basil of Caesarea, Gregory of Nyssa, Macrina (siblings) and their friend Gregory of Nazianzus. Cappadocia, comprising much of eastern Asia Minor, was largely a rural area with intermittent small towns and villages. The seats to which Basil appointed his brother and friend were anything but prestigious in the Byzantine imperial organization. Yet from that unlikely context, those four scholar/church persons/theologians came to dominate the mind of their century.

The method of the volume was not to deal with each author in sequence. Instead, Pelikan systematically organized a presentation of the views of the individual theologians around the focal questions, but did not hesitate to allow the four friends to disagree with each other. The exposition was presented in the flowing lucid style one has come to anticipate from Professor Pelikan. In nearly every instance, the quotations were artfully chosen from both the primary and secondary literature. Indeed, it will be interesting to observe how many salient quotations from Cappadocians and modern scholars will become standard features of later works!

Essential to reading the volume is an awareness of the structure (described by Pelikan, pp. 38-39). The first part of the volume examined the issues of theological language, the ways of knowing God, the unity and diversity of God, the universe as cosmos, space and time, the image of God, human divinization, the nature of good and eschatology from the perspective of "natural theology as apologetics." In the second part of the tome, these same issues, with some variations on themes, are approached from the perspective of "natural theology as presupposition." It is therefore advisable to read the corresponding chapters of the two sections in light of each other as well as within the sequence of the section in which they appear. No small task at that!

The thesis of the volume was that "the natural theology of the Cappadocians, and of the Greek Christian tradition as a total entity...was the product of...encounters with Hellenism (p. 21)." Pelikan argued that the central feature of the Cappadocian approach was "the language of negation" or *apophasis*. This understood the mystery of God to be the essential of God, and minimized the significance and accuracy of any positive affirmations which might be made about the nature and purpose of the divine. The main goal for humans, suggested the Cappadocians, was "Christian perfection," a notion already seen in the Qumran and biblical materials and especially with Alexandrian theology but with roots in Plato and Aristotle. Christian perfection was more than a restoration of the image of God according in creation. It sought also the achievement of the union of the human will with the divine will. These two foci of theological reflection, about humans and God, controlled the entire theological system of the Cappadocian writers.

Many of the particulars of Cappadocian theology will sound remarkably modern to most readers. For example, it was insisted that the attribution of gender to God was a human limitation and, as a matter of orthodoxy, God was beyond any ascription of gender. To assert the characteristic of gender to God, even in the ascription of "Father," is to approach the edge of heresy. With regard to abortion there was a difference of opinion: Basil considered abortion murder; Gregory of Nyssa understood a fetus as a potential human. With regard to eschatology, Basil insisted that the last judgment included condemnation. Gregory of Nyssa and Macrina argued for a universal restoration. Gregory of Nazianzus affirmed an Origenist hope for universal salvation.

While one hesitates to criticize such a magisterial effort, and with which one finds such resonance from one's own research, there are a number of concerns which do arise. The first is with regard to the influence of Origen of Alexandria. This writer, as Pelikan rightly suggested, was perhaps the major Christian theological influence on the development of Cappadocian thought (29-30, *et passim*). Pelikan properly indicated certain areas of agreement and disagreement of the fourth century writers with their third century Alexandrian/Caesarean predecessor. However, throughout Pelikan's analysis, the treatment would have been enriched by reference to Origen's thought. As it is, a careful analysis of the debt of the Cappadocians to Origen on the precise issues examined in the volume remains a desideratum. Part of the problem, with regard to Origen and to other early Christian materials is the unfortunately laconic footnote style, which takes up much space on the page but allows minimal possibility of allusion to relevant illuminatory materials.

Other issues are actually more central to the analysis. The assumption of both the Cambridge Platonists, on the one hand, and of Ritschl and von Harnack on the other, that there was a clear divergence between "gospel" and "hellenism" in earliest Christianity was perpetuated in the volume. Space does not allow a thorough critique of this thesis on the basis of extant early Christian texts, but suffice it to say that it would probably be more accurate to say that there was a divergence between popular hellenistic culture and the academic hellenistic culture encountered, understood and appropriated by Origen and the Cappadocians. Such a distinction would require a more nuanced analysis, an analysis complicated by the fact that Ephrem of Syria, contemporary of the Cappadocians, was making quite similar arguments about natural theology, the nature of God and the goal of humankind, all without direct recourse to academic Greek philosophy.

Secondly, the conflicts with the Arians and Manichaeans were minimally mentioned. Here Pelikan, and many other scholars, have taken their lead from the Cappadocians in not mentioning the names of certain opponents. The tradition of depriving one's enemies of free publicity, however, does not mean that the writers were ignorant of the challenges at hand. The Cappadocian's contemporary and intellectual fellow traveller, Ephrem, overtly developed his arguments in direct opposition to both Arians and Manichaeans, a fact which complicates Pelikan's picture of the Cappadocians. Thirdly, there is minimal discussion of the developments of academic philosophy either at Alexandria or at Athens and other centers. Most of the major writers of the period, including Plotinus and Porphyry, who had definitive influence on the philosophical possibilities appropriated by the Cappadocians, were not mentioned. Finally, significant research of the last two decades missed Pelikan's net. The traditional understanding of crucial elements of Cappadocian thought require nuancing because of the work of, for example, André de Halleux who was not mentioned.

Despite these shortcomings, Pelikan's analysis of the fourth century Cappadocian theologians is a major contribution to the history of Christian theology. It is to be hoped that this treatment of the theological background to the Nicene-Constantinopolitan Creed of 381 C.E. will add substance to the renewed interest in that landmark ecumenical creed, a document which institutionalized many of the theological conclusions of the Cappadocian writers, a statement promulgated by a Council of Constantinople initially convened under the presidency of none other than Gregory of Nazianzus.

DAVID BUNDY
Associate Professor of Church History
Christian Theological Seminary
Indianapolis, Indiana

McCoy, Charles S. and J. Wayne Baker, *Fountainhead of Federalism: Heinrich Bullinger and the Covenantal Tradition*, with a Translation of Bullinger's *Detestamento seu foedere Dei unico et aeterno* (1534). Westminster/John Knox Press: Louisville, Kentucky, 1991, 180 pp.

In recent years both theologians and political philosophers (particularly political philosophers who are interested in influences on the American Founding Fathers) have devoted attention to tracing the lines of influence of covenant thought in the realms of theology and governmental theory. For the first time to this reviewer's knowledge, these two trajectories, have been brought together in a single work. McCoy and Baker, both theologians, have competently traced the development of covenantal thought from its roots in the work of Heinrich Bullinger in the 16th century to its political adaptation in the thought of the American framers of the United States Constitution. Such an ambitious undertaking is accomplished in a book of only 98 pages, leaving the reader hungry for more but intrigued sufficiently to pursue the issue for himself in greater detail. Nevertheless, the authors have not in any way sacrificed accuracy by limiting the text. It is now commonly accepted that James Madison, the primary framer of the basic American legal document, the Constitution, was heavily influenced by men who were themselves influenced by "federal" thought, men such as John Witherspoon, John Locke, and David Hume.

Long before Madison, the Puritans of England and New England lived and moved in a covenantal world. McCoy and Baker take the reader on a fascinating journey back beyond the Puritans to the covenantal thought of Cocceius, well-known to theologians, and, in political philosophy, to Johannes Althusis, unknown to almost everyone. The fountainhead of this rich federal tradition is traced ultimately to the Swiss Reformer Bullinger. Covenant theology, as most theologians are aware, was a powerful organizing influence in sixteenth and seventeenth century Reformed theology. But the connection between this early covenant theology and later political thought has often been ignored or lost. McCoy and Baker have begun to remedy this situation in their work.

The authors have also done the theological world a huge favor by providing a translation of Bullinger's major work on the covenant, *De Testamento seu Foedere Dei unico et aeterno* (*On the One and Eternal Covenant of God*), published in 1534. If one is interested to know how covenant thought began in earnest, he must read this work preferably in the Latin, but at the very least, in this convenient translation.

If there are any criticisms of the book, the primary one is that the authors do not devote enough detail to the influences of federal thought on the American Founding Fathers. In general, the entire work could profitably be expanded. But, despite these shortcomings, if they can be so-called, this work is must reading. In addition, it contains a fairly comprehensive bibliography of covenant literature, primary and secondary. This reviewer would also recommend Baker's earlier work on Bullinger's covenant thinking, *Heinrich Bullinger and the Covenant: The Other Reformed Tradition.* (Athens, Ohio: Ohio University Press, 1980.)

MARC CLAUSON
Lexington Christian Academy
Lexington, Kentucky

Richey, Russell E., *Early American Methodism.* Bloomington and Indianapolis: Indiana University Press, 1991, xix, 137 pp. ISBN 0-253-35006-9.

*Early American Methodism* is a collection of six insightful essays, half of which originally appeared in different form in *Methodist History.* Russell E. Richey, research professor of church history at Duke University Divinity School, is a honed essayist capable of distilling vast amounts of secondary literature for the non-specialist, and, following the "principle of fecudity," suggesting new lines of interpretation. Religious history typically appears in the fuller dress of the narrative, yet the linkage of Methodism and the essay form seems highly appropriate given John Wesley's fondness for the sermonic essay, his chief means of theologizing. Much of the evidence Richey musters—personal journals and meditations—would, in less deft hands, seem merely arbitrary and anecdotal. Considering his ability to find much where little appears to the untrained eye, Richey seems possessed of the same "glass to the heart" (p. 44) that animated Francis Asbury.

Richey understands his work to be "self-consciously a revisionist endeavor" (p. xi), executed in the narrow confines of forty years, 1770-1810. It is a rare work of history that is at once both avowedly revisionist and yet discerning of and sympathetic toward the religious sensibilities of the phenomena in question. Revisionist history is almost by definition reductionist history, dismissing religion as vestigial. The revisionism on display here is enriching, not denuding, for it clarifies much of Methodism's original intent in America, namely, "To reform the Continent, and to spread scriptural Holiness over these lands" (p. 36). Richey's clarity is not simply cleaning an old lens grown dusty with time, but a fresh lens ground in part by contemporary concerns, that illumines the past and suggests how it can in turn illumine the future. It is a subtle clarity, turning on evidence such as two words highlighted here and a preposition substituted for a conjunction there. On such subtleties hangs the "Methodist construction of reality" (p.79) that Richey builds. When Bishop William McKendree changes Wesley's two-pronged dictum of reforming the continent *and* spreading scriptural holiness to reforming *by* spreading scriptural holiness (pp. 35, 61), Richey overturns the conventional interpretation that saw reform being collapsed into evangelism. Reform, for Richey, cannot be a competitor to holiness. In the early national period under review, Methodists "had a very powerful corporate purpose and did, in fact, offer a model of a reformed continent" (p. 62).

In what was almost an aside in the journals of eighteenth-century Methodist preachers, "We rode" (p. 8), Richey again finds very nearly an entire world, a world of community that overturns a cherished idol of Methodist—and American—individualism: "the solitary, cloaked horseman, braving storm and cold...to deliver the gospel" (p. 8). Most often those paired riders were Southerners, as Richey shows in perhaps the most engaging essay, "The Southern Accent of American Methodism." In the South, early Methodism proposed "an evangelical alternative to patriarchal Anglicanism" (p. 55), built the church biracially, showed profound ambivalence toward slavery, and dramatized grace in public gatherings, especially the quarterly conference and later the annual conference. Here Richey makes the claim never before heard that "the South shaped American religion as a whole" (p. 50), although Methodism has largely ignored its Southern roots. Overcoming the New England bias for religious beginnings is not easy. The choir director in Thornton Wilder's *Our Town* charged his New Hampshire Congregational choristers to stifle their loud singing. That should be left to the Methodists.

Richey's early American Methodism is not bawdy or unseemly, but certainly full-throated. "We need a rewritten version of Methodist history, seen from the bottom up" (p. 53). Looking from the bottom-up vantage, three realities—community, fraternity, and order—gave to Methodism "incredible power" (p. 13) when properly balanced. Community eventuated in feasts of love, fraternity happened especially among the travelling preachers who rode in pairs, and order carried forth the scriptural episcopacy that Americans inherited from Wesley's Anglicanism. There is almost a triune premise at work among community, fraternity, and order, for within the Trinity, although of infinite and not measurable span, there is also "the ordering of the spiritual resources of each for the sake of the whole connection and ultimately the king-dom" (p. 13).

The final essay, "The Four Languages of Early American Methodism," is not only a cul-mination but also a model for writing denominational history. Every denomination has its own linguistic structure, its preferred "grammar of grace." Richey testifies to the efficacy of the first Methodist language, the popular or evangelical, every time he cites a journal entry from Francis Asbury, Jesse Lee, or others. The popular language connected Methodists with revival-minded Presbyterians and Baptists. Revival, "predominantly a communal affair" (p. 3), sometimes erupted with no preacher present. John Wesley, however pleased he might have been with the popular or evangelical language, spoke more directly and doctrinally in the second language Richey identifies, the Wesleyan. It was not only the language of the warm heart, but also of the clear mind. The third language, the episcopal or Anglican, might seem a simple reiteration of the Wesleyan, but Richey claims that these two lan-guages, certainly capable of juxtaposition, were "not really conceptually unified" (p. 92). These two languages might be spoken at the same annual conference, although at different times for different reasons. The fourth language, the republican, was spoken most clearly by James O'Kelly, who formed the Republican Methodist Church in 1792 when that year's General Conference denied his motion to give preachers the right to contest the bishop's appointment of them. Perhaps only the episodic Methodists could continue to speak four languages without blending them into one, as did the Lutherans and Calvinists. But every denomination will be found to speak many voices, not unlike the requirement to show the church's four classic marks: unity, holiness, apostolicity, catholicity.

It is said that short stories are harder to write than novels, and historical essays presum-ably exact greater labor than narratives. *Early American Methodism* shows both the essay form and its practitioner at their best. Only occasionally does Richey transgress John Wesley's "a plain truth for plain people" criterion. Only occasionally is slender evidence made to support more than it really can. If this revisionist history is written from the bot-tom up, it ends at a kind of summit, allowing one to see early Methodist standards like the camp meeting and the quarterly conference in a truer, more bracing light.

RODERICK T. LEUPP
Visiting Professor of Theology
Asia-Pacific Nazarene Theological Seminary
Metro Manila, Philippines

Gill, Kenneth D., *Toward a Contextualized Theology for the Third World* (Studies in the Intercultural Theology of Christianity, 90 pp.; Frankfurt am Main: Peter Lang, 1994). xi, 311 pp. ISBN 3-631-47096-7.

This volume traces the historical and theological developments of one of the major Pentecostal traditions in Mexico as it formulated an understanding and praxis of

Christianity which was contextualized in a particular "Third World" milieu. The book is the final stage of a dissertation presented at the University of Birmingham, England, written under the direction of Prof. Walter Hollenweger. Gill is presently Collection Development Librarian at The Billy Graham Center Library, Wheaton College. Previously, he held positions at the Asbury Theological Seminary and University of Texas-El Paso Libraries.

The Pentecostal tradition studied here is known by various names: "Jesus Name," "Jesus Only," or "Oneness" Pentecostalism. The perspective arose in the early years of the Pentecostal tradition when it was noticed at a camp-meeting at Arroyo Seco, California, that the New Testament instructions to baptize, with the exception of Matthew 28:19, all talked of baptism "in Jesus' name" rather than with the traditional trinitarian formula. This liturgical observation led to a permanent division between "Trinitarian" Pentecostals and "Oneness" Pentecostals, a difference of perspective which has become more pronounced through the conflict and intellectual posturing of both sides. The "Oneness" perspective has become primarily, with the exception of the United Pentecostal Church, a tradition of Hispanic and African-American churches in the United States, and an important branch of Pentecostalism outside the U.S.A., especially in Mexico.

The first chapter (pp. 1-42) discusses the origins of "Jesus' Name Pentecostalism" tracing its development from the Arroyo Seco Camp-meeting through the formation of the Assemblies of God (from its beginnings anti-Oneness) and the U.S.A. "Oneness" denominations, the Pentecostal Assemblies of the World and the United Pentecostal Church.

The second chapter (pp. 43-74) describes the development of the "Jesus' Name Movement" in Mexico. During 1912, Romanita, a young Mexican woman, was converted at a small house church in Los Angeles. In 1914, after the end of the Mexican civil war, Romanita returned to Mexico, and with the assistance of her nephew, Miguel Garcia, began Bible studies. One of the converts was a Methodist Holiness pastor Ruben Ortega, who before he took over leadership of the new "*Iglesia Apostólica*," was rebaptized in "Jesus' Name" in southern Texas. From this modest beginning, the new movement spread throughout Mexico and into the United States where a separate denomination was organized in 1930. As with most of the Pentecostal and/or Holiness churches, these all divided, generally over issues of leadership and organization, to form other related groups.

The struggle for organization and theological unity within the framework of evolving contextualization in Mexican culture is described in chapter three (pp. 75-116). Never dominated by foreign missionaries or mission organizations, the *Iglesia Apostólica* was able to decide which foreign elements would be a part of its liturgy, theology, and praxis. Importantly, its clergy, theologians, and other leaders were never the paid staff of foreign organizations. It was a church of the lower and lower middle classes with an indigenous leadership, frequently of worker-pastors.

Although it is not thus presented by Gill, much of the rest of the story of the denomination is the history of a remarkable family, the Gaxiola family which is now entering its third generation of leadership in the church. Maclovio Gaxiola Lopez established (1943) the *Liberia Latinoamericana* as the publishing house of the *Iglesia Apostólica*. He took over publication of the periodical *El Mensajero Apostólica*, which in 1943 became *El Eségeta*. Interested in education both of ministers and clergy, he organized the first Bible schools. In 1948, his son Manuel J. Gaxiola began to publish a Sunday School curriculum which evolved into *Espositor Biblico Cristiano*. In the midst of his pastoral, educational and publishing responsibilities, Maclovio Gaxiola published a systematic theology, *Teología Moral: Doctrina y Disciplina Cristiana* (Mexico, D.F.: Librería Apostólica, 1962) which for the first time offered a comprehensive systematic treatment of the Apostolic theological perspective. This was followed by a history of the church: *Historia de la Iglesia Apostólica de la Fe en Cristo Jesús* (Mexico, D.F.: Librería Apostólica, 1964).

The second section of the volume describes the process of theological development. Beginning with a description of early Christian theology (perhaps the weakest part of the volume), Gill narrates the development of "Oneness" theology in the U.S.A. before moving to a perhaps too brief discussion of the Mexican context in chapter six (pp. 177-198). Here, on the basis of materials published by the *Iglesia Apostólica* and interviews, Gill presents a narrative of the development of the theological perspective of the tradition as it has wrestled with the harmonization of the liturgical, christological, and trinitarian doctrines. He argues that the theologians of the *Iglesia Apostólica* have found ways to state these doctrines which are within the framework established by the ante-Nicene church and that are not incompatible with trends in contemporary theology. In this theological effort, Manuel Gaxiola has been the major constructive theologian. As a theologian, ecumenist, and historian, he builds upon the base of his father's work and has published an impressive list of scholarly books and articles, thirty of which are listed in Gill's bibliography. Most of the anonymous official documents of the church also reflect significant, often determinative input from Manuel Gaxiola and his father. Manuel Gaxiola, who also earned a doctorate at the University of Birmingham under Hollenweger, is certainly one of the most prolific Pentecostal historians and theologians.

The appendices to the book provide important organizational and credal documents, as well as information about two splinter denominations, the *Iglesia Evangélica Cristiana Espiritel* and *La Luz del Mundo*. The classified bibliography will be an indispensable resource for scholarship on Mexican Pentecostalism and the index facilitates access to the tome.

Gill's volume presents a carefully documented case study of theological development within one "Third World" context which is both interesting and important. The *Iglesia Apostólica* has grown into one of the largest Mexican non-Catholic denominations. As such, it is a model for other traditions seeking to shed the vestiges of European and U.S.A. cultural structures in light of their own reading and living of the biblical narratives. The book will be an essential source for discussing the development of Pentecostalism and the Holiness Movement outside the U.S.A.

DAVID BUNDY
Associate Professor of Church History
Christian Theological Seminary
Indianapolis, Indiana

Poewe, Karla, ed., *Charismatic Christianity as a Global Culture* (Studies in Comparative Religion; Columbia, SC: University of South Carolina Press, 1994). xiv, 300 pp.

This is a major effort to describe and analyze a reality apparent to observers of global Christianity; that is that the traditions first defined by the religious expressions of the Mediterranean, Reformation, and North American mainline experience are being circumvented or challenged by a new tradition, Pentecostalism. If David Barratt's statistics (*Dictionary of Pentecostal and Charismatic Movements* (Grand Rapids: Zondervan, 1988) are anywhere close to accurate, even in a comparative sense, Pentecostalism and the Charismatic groups have come to be the second largest Christian communion after Roman Catholicism. The volume, edited by Karla Poewe, professor of anthropology at the University of Calgary, is comprised of a collection of 11 essays by an international team of 10 specialists in anthropology and religious studies.

The introduction by K. Poewe, exploring "the nature, globality and history of Charismatic Christianity," provides a phenomenological description of the data, asserts its global expanse citing relevant sources, and attempts to provide a narrative of the process of this expansion. This is probably the most problematic section of the book. To take Chinese Christianity, for instance, *directly* from Jesuits and Pietists, to current expressions of charismatic Christianity in China, without any attention to the American and British mission efforts of the late nineteenth and twentieth centuries and their encounter with Pentecostalism, which has been documented by Daniel Bays, among others, is not historically accurate. The influence of the independent, denominational or para-church Holiness and Pentecostal missions never enters into the discussion.

It is not that this experience, which had established its own global dimension before World War I, should be determinative for the interpretation of the whole, or that the traditions, as they now stand, have not grown far beyond any American or European beginnings. However, this lack of attention to the contribution of the American experience of the nineteenth and twentieth centuries as well as the complete lack of attention to European contributions, especially from England, Italy, and Scandinavia, to the development of Pentecostalism and/or Charismatic religion seriously mars the book. It is highly improbable that early Pentecostal missionaries were aware of M. Ricci, K.F. Gützlaff, or even J. Gossner. It is certain that they knew Phoebe Palmer, William Taylor, Sadar Sundu Singh, Charles Parham, William Seymour, Oral Roberts, Jimmy Swaggert, William Branham, and Gordon Lindsay, as well as T.B. Barratt, W.F.P. Burton, Lewi Pethrus, and Reinhard Bonnke. More appropriate is the emphasis on the "faith mission" tradition of Müller and James Hudson Taylor who did become "icons" for the traditions.

This reviewer would want to argue with Poewe that Pietism had an important influence on the development of Pentecostalism, but that it was filtered through the American and European Holiness and Pentecostal experience. After it was exported, the nexus of ideas and methods which are part of these spiritual traditions, achieved a life of their own. The American and European Holiness and Pentecostal experience liberated, for better or worse, the ideas of personal piety accompanied by an empirically verifiable response to the perception of the presence of God in the believer's life and the accompanying need for "social holiness" from the necessity of direct connection to established ecclesiastical traditions. Thus for example, in Latin America and Africa, the "Charismatic religion" did not originate with the results of German Lutheran mission, but developed quite apart from these churches with primary impetus from other traditions. In Poewe's defense, however, it must be said that scholars of Pentecostalism in its global forms have often forgotten the complex European heritage which lies behind their own ideas. Poewe's formulation may help us to work toward a more adequate understanding of the tradition.

The first section of the volume deals with methods and models. André Droogers, University of Amsterdam, explores from a sociological perspective, "why and in what sense religious experiences are or are not normal (p. 3)." Irving Hexham and K. Poewe present an enlightening study analyzing how the Pentecostal and Charismatic churches in South Africa were treated by both the media and by the extreme right and left position in the *apartheid* struggle.

The second section contains articles on Latin America (David Martin), a groundbreaking study of Korean Pentecostal Missions to Japan (Mark A. Mullins, Meiji Gakuin University, Tokyo) which suggests many new avenues of research, and a review of the discussions about the relationship between Pentecostalism and Fundamentalism by Russell Spittler.

The third section explores the process by which "orality" was turned into "literary narrative." Charles Nienkirchen contributes an important essay in which are described the "conflicting visions of the past" in the "prophetic use of history in the early American Pentecostal-Charismatic movements (p. 119)." The essay by Nancy Schwartz is a pioneering analysis of the Legio Maria, a large independent "charismatic" Catholic church in western Kenya and Tanzania where she has done research since 1982 and related to her still unpublished Princeton Ph.D. dissertation. Stanley Johannesen, University of Waterloo, presented case studies on the development of "third generation Pentecostal Language (pp. 175-199)," which attempts to suggest alternatives to the influential analysis of Jean-Daniel Pluss based on Riccour and literary theory.

Walter Hollenweger, professor emeritus, University of Birmingham, contributed an important article directed more toward Pentecostals in the so-called "first world" than to anthropologists and sociologists. He deplores the tendency to "ruthlessly" transform oral narratives to written forms which become exclusionary rather than inclusionary. He insists that "privileged Pentecostals and scholars must learn to speak in, and listen to stories (p. 200)."

The final essays in the section entitled "Charismatic Christian Thought," were contributed by G. Roelofs, graduate student at the University of Amsterdam, who examines the use of orality and language in Flemish (Belgian) charismatic groups, and by Karla Poewe who, in an extremely important methodological and programmatic article, urges a "rethinking [of] the relationship of anthropology to science and religion." This chapter alone is worth the price of the volume.

This volume is indeed a *tour de force*. Each essay is a significant contribution to understanding religious life in the contemporary world. It models a multi-disciplinary approach to the study of Pentecostalism and Charismatic Christianity and removes it from the exclusive province of historians and theologians. Quite appropriately, historians and theologians will need to be aware of the theories and analytical results of sociological and anthropological study. These can probably be brought to new levels of sophistication by an awareness of the diachronic narrative of the tradition being studied. As Poewe suggests, those inside and outside the traditions can make complementary contributions to the study of this very interesting, complicated, and multi-layered expression of religious beliefs.

DAVID BUNDY
Associate Professor of Church History
Christian Theological Seminary
Indianapolis, Indiana